Praise for *Pathway to Teaching*

"*Pathway to Teaching* is a must-read for teacher candidates of all ages. As a high school Teacher Academy teacher, I appreciate having a text that is current, informative, and written in student-friendly language. Although this book was not written specifically for high school students, Dr. Hougan takes what can be considered information overload and breaks it into practical chunks that promote great class discussion."

—**Carla Smith**, Teacher Academy Coordinator

"Eric Hougan has created a blueprint for success in *Pathway to Teaching*. Each section is outlined with easy-to-implement strategies that will carry you throughout your entire journey from college to career. Packed with insightful and in-depth looks on everything from self-care to interview preparation to networking (and much more), this book is a must-have guide for anyone entering the field of education."

—**Leann Schumacher**, teacher

"Dr. Hougan speaks to the complexity and demands of becoming a teacher. If any teacher candidate is aiming to thrive in their preparation program, rather than just survive, *Pathway to Teaching* is the guide to help them navigate through the process. Hougan's strategies, tips, and systems go beyond the teacher preparation program. He sets future teachers up for success without burning themselves out before they ever enter their classrooms."

—**Nicolette Moser**, teacher

"Dr. Hougan has written the best book for anyone considering teaching as a career. If you want to be prepared for it all, read this book!"

—**Brieanna Lutes**, teacher

"Being a teacher is as hard as it is rewarding. Becoming a teacher is getting harder everyday. With this guide, Hougan makes the process much easier to understand and accomplish successfully. If you're considering teaching as a career, this is a must-read."

—**Robert Hand**, 2019 WA State Teacher of the Year

"A must-read for teacher candidates needing to succeed in their program and secure the ideal teaching job!"

—**Alexis Rios**, teacher

Pathway to Teaching

Pathway to Teaching

A Guide to Teacher Training, Student Teaching, and Finding a Job

Eric Hougan

ROWMAN & LITTLEFIELD
Lanham • Boulder • New York • London

Published by Rowman & Littlefield
An imprint of The Rowman & Littlefield Publishing Group, Inc.
4501 Forbes Boulevard, Suite 200, Lanham, Maryland 20706
www.rowman.com

6 Tinworth Street, London SE11 5AL, United Kingdom

Copyright © 2020 by Eric Hougan

All rights reserved. No part of this book may be reproduced in any form or by any electronic or mechanical means, including information storage and retrieval systems, without written permission from the publisher, except by a reviewer who may quote passages in a review.

British Library Cataloguing in Publication Information Available

Library of Congress Cataloging-in-Publication Data

Names: Hougan, Eric, author.
Title: Pathway to teaching : a guide to teacher training, student teaching, and finding a job / Eric Hougan.
Other titles: Road to teaching
Description: Lanham : Rowman & Littlefield, [2020] | Revised edition of: Road to teaching : a guide to teacher training, student teaching and finding a job. Charleston, SC : Booksurge, [2008]. | Summary: "Pathway to Teaching demystifies becoming an educator by providing strategies to aspiring teachers at each crucial stage: teacher training, student teaching, and finding a job. The presented strategies address a range of topics from the edTPA – a nationwide teacher assessment – to classroom management approaches, to ideas on self-care"—Provided by publisher.
Identifiers: LCCN 2019046539 (print) | LCCN 2019046540 (ebook) | ISBN 9781475847444 (cloth) | ISBN 9781475847451 (paperback) | ISBN 9781475847468 (epub)
Subjects: LCSH: Teaching—Vocational guidance—United States. | Teachers—Training of—United States. | Teaching—United States. | Teachers—Employment—United States.
Classification: LCC LB1775.2 .H686 2020 (print) | LCC LB1775.2 (ebook) | DDC 371.102023—dc23
LC record available at https://lccn.loc.gov/2019046539
LC ebook record available at https://lccn.loc.gov/2019046540

Contents

Foreword	ix
Preface	xi
Acknowledgments	xiii
Introduction	xv

SECTION I: LEVERAGE YOUR TEACHER EDUCATION TRAINING — 1

1	Understanding the Teaching Process	3
2	Save and Organize Information with Purpose	6
3	Organize Your Reading	9
4	Journal to Reflect and Organize Your Thoughts	11
5	Organize for the edTPA™	14
6	Prioritize Self-Care	16
7	A Novice Teacher's Perspective: Growth Comes from Imperfection	21
8	Differentiate Yourself Through Education	22
9	Become an Expert on a Particular Concept	24
10	Address Your Growth Areas	26
11	Benefit from Networking in Schools	28

12	Get Face Time with Administrators	30
13	Network within Your Teacher Education Program	31
14	Consider Everyone Part of Your Network	32
15	Organize Your Contacts	33

SECTION II: EXCEL AT STUDENT TEACHING — 35

16	Develop Your Philosophy and Core Values	37
17	Proclaim Your Student Teaching Goals	41
18	Research the Community, School, and Students	44
19	Keep Abreast of Your Field	47
20	Communicate Early with Your Cooperating Teacher	49
21	Working with Your Cooperating Teacher	52
22	A Cooperating Teacher's Perspective: Advice for Student Teachers	54
23	Tackling the edTPA	56
24	A University Field Supervisor's Perspective: edTPA Tips from the Field	58
25	Get Your Feet Wet Early On	60
26	Learn Names Quickly	62
27	Be Outstanding Inside and Outside of the Classroom	65
28	Use Classroom Management to Your Advantage	68
29	Know Yourself When It Comes to Discipline	75
30	Think Customer Service	78
31	Build Your Touchstone	81
32	How to Approach the edTPA Writing	85
33	Thank Your Network	88

SECTION III: FIND YOUR IDEAL TEACHER JOB — 91

34	Continue to Shine After Student Teaching	93
35	Craft an Effective Résumé	96

36	A Career Counselor's Perspective: Career Advice	101
37	Ask (the Right Person) for Help on Your Résumé	102
38	Learn from Your Work Experience	104
39	Be Aware of the Hiring Time Frame	106
40	Jump-Start Your Job Search	108
41	Attend Education Career Fairs and District Open Houses	110
42	Draw from Your Network	112
43	Track Your Job Search	113
44	Leverage Your Research	115
45	Framing Your Response to Interview Questions	118
46	Practice Interview Questions	122
47	Control the Interview Process	125
48	Go for a Trial Run	130
49	Dress to Impress	132
50	Hit a Home Run	134
51	A Principal's Perspective: A Passion to Teach	136
Appendix		137
About the Contributors		143
About the Author		145

Foreword

Tina H. Boogren

This book that you're holding in your hands is the *exact* book that my younger self so desperately needed. As the first person in my family to enter into the world of teaching, I felt lost trying to navigate through my teacher prep program, the precarious world of student teaching, and applying for my first teaching position. If I had had this book, the pathway would have been much less daunting and so much more inviting.

As an advocate and supporter of beginning teachers, I've contributed to the field by providing resources for those first few years in the classroom. What Eric Hougan has so brilliantly done here is to fill in an often overlooked but essentially vital part of the pathway to teaching—guidance around the three pivotal stages that a teacher candidate must navigate *before* becoming a teacher. And he's the perfect person to have by your side. As an associate professor in education, Dr. Hougan is on the front lines with teacher candidates every single day and is one of the biggest teacher advocates in the field today. He is able to lean into those experiences to provide concrete strategies to help navigate each stage of the journey. As you embark on your path to becoming a teacher, you'll feel such gratitude that you have Dr. Hougan's book by your side, guiding and cheering you on.

While I wholeheartedly agree with and support *every* essential strategy found in this book, I especially love the emphasis on self-care and the importance of taking care of ourselves so that we can take care of our students. As Dr. Hougan states, "Every child deserves an educator that is present, rested, positive, and passionate about the work," and I couldn't agree more with this proclamation. I urge you to take this strategy seriously and commit to embracing imperfection, setting boundaries, forming healthy habits, and continuing to prioritize your understanding of teacher wellness and self-care, as this will serve you for your entire career as an educator.

I am excited for you to begin your journey with *Pathway to Teaching* as your guidebook, and I welcome you to this wonderful world of education! You're going to love it here!

Preface

Congratulations on choosing a career in education. Your journey to becoming a teacher will be both rewarding and challenging. Along the way, you will witness your own dramatic growth, both personally and professionally. In the end, you will be a teacher. Through hard work and perseverance, you will positively impact the lives of individuals and future generations.

My journey to becoming a teacher was a long one. When I was younger, my passion was for business. As a college student, I worked full-time and quickly climbed the business ladder. Upon college graduation, I traveled to India, where I took a position as a project manager in a startup company. I was quickly achieving my career and financial goals. But a piece of me was not satisfied.

The part of my job that I found most satisfying was speaking to the groups of new hires. At every opportunity, I would drop everything and run to greet new hires before they started their training. I remember how they always looked nervous but eager to learn. Over time I spent more and more time in the training classrooms and finally began conducting my own classes. I was thrilled to watch them transform into capable and successful employees. Witnessing the growth of individuals was more rewarding than money or titles.

Looking back, this was the moment I was called to teach. I returned to the United States to become a teacher, combining my passion for business with teaching. My goal was to teach business to high school students. After some research, I applied to an established teacher education program, but this was just the beginning of my journey. My head swirled with questions about my new chosen profession. I searched for hours on the Internet to determine what certification I needed, which classes I was required to take, and how much a beginning teacher would earn. I became frustrated culling through this information; I deeply wished for a single resource to guide me through the process of becoming a teacher.

The limited resources I did find for soon-to-be teachers was fragmented and usually focused on a single subject, such as interviewing. It was further apparent the vast majority of books I read dealt with the experiences of first-year teachers, not future teachers.

In my path to becoming a teacher, I decided that this fragmented information needed to be consolidated into an easy-to-read information book. Therefore, when I was pursuing my master's degree in education, to become a teacher, I began to collect information, resources, tips, and strategies to create a single resource for soon-to-be teachers. This research was the genesis for this book. *Pathway to Teaching* aims to share pertinent information in a meaningful way with the thousands of future teachers—to provide a helpful pathway, of sorts, for those entering the profession.

Acknowledgments

Special thanks are due to all the people that contributed their thoughts, advice, and guidance, especially Judy Longstreth, Angela Engel, and Cris Welch. In particular, I am deeply appreciative of Leann Schumacher for her invaluable feedback and support in writing this book. Last, but not least, I am appreciative to my family, friends, teachers, colleagues, and students who have greatly influenced me throughout the years.

Introduction

The intended audience for this book is anyone who is interested in becoming a teacher. Throughout the book, the term "teacher candidate" will be used to indicate an individual actively pursuing a teaching career. A teacher candidate typically goes through three pivotal phases before becoming a certified teacher: attending a teacher education preparation program, completing a practicum (student teaching), and conducting a job search. This book is organized into three sections, addressing each of these important phases with specific strategies.

The topics of the strategies vary widely. Presented strategies may range from addressing the new reality of the edTPA assessment, to providing ideas on self-care, to developing your philosophy and core values regarding education, to setting yourself up for a successful teacher interview. Yet, common themes emerge throughout the entire book that center on *organization*, *networking*, and *differentiation*. By attending to these essential themes and applying the strategies, you will be in a better position to leverage your teacher education training, excel at student teaching, and find your ideal teaching job.

Section I

LEVERAGE YOUR TEACHER EDUCATION TRAINING

Chapter 1

Understanding the Teaching Process

"Change is the law of life and those who look only to the past or present are certain to miss the future."—John F. Kennedy

In education nothing is static; change is the one constant factor. To survive you need to embrace this reality, as your pedagogy will be challenged regularly by new students, research, and ideas. This begs the question: How does a novice teacher tackle the challenge of constant change? In short, teachers need to continually adapt and reinvent themselves as professionals. This transformation is a process of acquiring knowledge about new changes and how to best address them; applying this knowledge; and, finally, reflecting upon how well you, as a teacher, met these changes.

BUILDING A FOUNDATION OF KNOWLEDGE

In the first stage of your teacher training, you will be a learner, building a foundation of knowledge with your studies, research, practice, experiences, and reflection. Here are a few ways you may grow as a learner in your educational training:

- Observing classrooms,
- Diving into the history and laws of education,
- Creating lesson plans that address students' learning needs,
- Learning about culturally responsive teaching,
- Experimenting with instruction and assessment to meet students' diverse learning needs,
- Integrating technology into the learning environment,

- Developing a deeper understanding of the education lexicon,
- And much more.

Through your studies and experiences, you will begin to establish the necessary foundation to build your teaching philosophy and pedagogy. By continually seeking knowledge, possessing the courage to apply best practices, and developing a habit of meaningful self-reflection, not only will you keep pace with change but you will also become a catalyst for positive change.

APPLYING YOUR KNOWLEDGE

The next step in the teaching process is the application of knowledge: taking all that you have learned and applying it in the classroom. For a teacher candidate, student teaching is the culminating practicum experience that allows you to practice what you have learned throughout your teacher training within a real classroom.

Even before student teaching, a teacher candidate may have opportunities to apply their knowledge and skills. Traditional teacher preparation programs are shifting to increase opportunities for practice, specifically by integrating more fieldwork within the schools. Yet, even if opportunities to be in the schools are limited, you may experience opportunities for practice by lesson planning, teaching your peers, developing the habit of listening to constructive criticism, and learning from your mistakes with your teacher training.

The application of knowledge is a critical piece in the teaching process. You must be open to new ideas, paradigms, and pedagogical best practices, and be willing to challenge yourself to apply those in your classroom. In the application stage, you begin to define yourself as a teacher who takes risks and puts forth his or her best effort.

REFLECTION ON CONTINUAL IMPROVEMENT

In the spirit of continual improvement, you will be doing a great deal of reflection as a teacher and a teacher candidate. A reflective teacher focuses on areas of growth and celebration, continuously looks to the future, and is driven to excel. Reflection allows you to evaluate the effectiveness of your pedagogy during the application stage. In other words, you will examine what worked and what didn't work, such as trying a new instructional strategy or strengthening student relationships. Furthermore, through this reflective lens, you will consider the changes needed for the future, as this reflective process is an ongoing commitment to renewal and growth.

Reflecting on your pedagogy should not be burdensome or time-consuming. Sometimes just jotting down quick notes on what you wish to improve is sufficient. The main point is to find a system that allows you to adjust and improve your lessons. Practical strategies on becoming a more reflective teacher are provided later in the book. By learning from your experiences, you will continue to build your foundation of knowledge and the teaching process will continue.

Chapter 2

Save and Organize Information with Purpose

"The trouble with organizing a thing is that pretty soon folks get to paying more attention to the organization than to what they're organized for."—Laura Ingalls Wilder

During your teaching training, you will receive a large amount of information from a variety of sources—instructors, peers, and your personal experiences—on everything from special education to bilingual education to school reform. At times, you will feel overwhelmed by it all. For example, one teacher candidate described how he was handed over sixty articles on twenty different topics in just one academic quarter, which led him to feel like he was collapsing under the information overload. Hence, organizing your information with purpose will effectively build your knowledge foundation and help to keep you from feeling overloaded and overwhelmed by the constant stream of information you will be receiving. Your organization system should also allow you to easily access and reference this pertinent information any time you wish to use it in the future.

Furthermore, developing the ability to capture information and gather personal meaning from it will not only help you to work more efficiently, but it is also a valuable skill you can teach to your students once you have mastered it. Being organized with purpose allows you to better recall information quickly, and, more importantly, be able to extract meaningful knowledge from it.

CREATE YOUR ORGANIZATION STRUCTURE

An effective organization strategy can save you a lot of future frustration. Start by developing a filing system. Keep in mind that in order for you to organize with purpose, the filing system you choose should work for you and your specific needs. If using a physical system of file folders, be sure they mirror your electronic system, so you can easily access information in either place. For both your physical and electronic materials, consider the following file structures:

- Create course folders and save the materials in their respective course folder.
- Develop folders based on themes. For instance, perhaps you have written about social justice issues in several classes. Instead of saving each piece of work in each separate class folder, it might be easier to save all works regarding social justice in one folder named "Social Justice."
- Establish folders based on your teacher education activities or administrative materials. For example, you might want to save all your classroom observation notes in one folder, regardless of which class you completed them for.

Next, attempt to go entirely digital, as having the majority of your materials in electronic format has its advantages. The chief advantage is accessibility: You will be able to access your materials virtually anywhere as long as you have your phone, tablet, laptop, or computer. To streamline this process, try to get all your information (syllabi, research papers, etc.) electronically. If you receive physical copies (and no electronic versions are available), digitize these materials by scanning the materials using a printer/copier or other scanning devices (e.g., ScanSnap). Another way is to download a scanning app to your phone or tablet. These apps, typically free or low-cost, utilize your phone's camera to take photos of your materials and convert them to electronic documents (for example, PDFs), which you can save to your files.

Another consideration when designing your organization system is how you are going to back up your materials. Take advantage of the various "cloud" data-storage solutions in the market (for example, Dropbox, Google Drive, iCloud, etc.). Using a cloud-based data provider allows you to save a (local) copy to your device; the service simultaneously saves several copies to their secure servers, often located around the world. This ensures that your data cannot be lost and is accessible from anywhere.

Alternatively, you could use applications that can scan materials while also being cloud-based. The features of these applications, such as Evernote, Microsoft's OneNote, and Google's Keep, allow you to create notes, capture images, create PDFs, and tag your notes (super helpful for capturing themes); they also provide you with robust search capabilities.

ADD HELPFUL NOTES

While you may have your organizational filing system firmly in place, there is still the problem of having too little time to sift through so many papers. Imagine you are in your first year of teaching. You have a student who has a learning disability, and you want to read up on that specific disability to determine if there are approaches you can take to address the student's needs. Remembering that you have some research from your teacher training program, you go to a file labeled "Exceptional Students." There are over a dozen articles and research packets in the folder. You do not have the time to read or even review each article to search for that specific learning disability your student may have.

An extremely effective way of avoiding this problem is to add notes to each article or research packet that you receive. As you review an article in class, take a moment to jot down some notes on the article's thesis and any meaningful points that might be of use in the future. You can write your notes on the article's cover page, or on a sticky note. Here are a few sentence starters to help you write concise, useful notes:

- "The purpose of this article is…"
- "The big idea is…"
- "This article is meaningful because…"
- "My takeaways as a future teacher are…"

Develop this organizational strategy into a habit, not a chore, by avoiding the temptation to write extensive notes on each article you receive. Rather, write something quick and succinct that will help to jog your memory, so in the future when you are searching your files you can quickly recall whether the article will be able to assist you in your inquiry or not. This strategy will be immensely useful throughout your teaching career as you push yourself to synthesize information while it is still fresh and therefore continue to build a meaningful knowledge foundation for future applications.

Chapter 3

Organize Your Reading

"Reading is essential for those who seek to rise above the ordinary."
—Jim Rohn

Educators are expected to stay abreast of current research, and doing so means that you will be reading books and scholarly papers on a regular basis. As a teacher candidate, it is wise to organize your reading as you go along by writing a list of all the relevant books and articles you have read on education. The list of reading should include:

- Title of the book/paper
- Author(s) name
- Subject matter
- Application to teaching (e.g., methodology, classroom management, etc.)

Under each entry, write a short synopsis of the work (your big takeaways) and how it might apply to your teaching. Again, consider saving your reading list electronically, preferably using one of the cloud-based note-taking apps such as Evernote or Google Keep. You may also want to add your reading list to an online book review site, for example, GoodReads (https://www.goodreads.com/). Be sure to use a public profile setting so that anyone searching for you on the Internet, such as a school recruiter, may view your reading list, thereby signaling to them your interest and motivation for professional excellence.

Maintaining a professional reading list has several advantages. For instance, you may be asked in an interview to discuss some education-related literature you have recently read. This interview question is especially common for reading-intensive teaching positions, such as language arts. Before your interview, you can refresh your memory by briefly reviewing your reading list and noting some of the books and articles that have made the biggest impact on you or your pedagogy.

Finally, this comprehensive reading list will serve as your professional reference library. Suppose that after three years of teaching you have to teach a class that includes a student with autism. You recall reading a book that might shed a great deal of insight on teaching students with special needs, especially in regards to the intricacies of educating children who are on the autism spectrum. By simply referring to your reading list, you will quickly discover the author and title of the book, thus giving you the ability to efficiently access the information needed.

Chapter 4

Journal to Reflect and Organize Your Thoughts

"By three methods we may learn wisdom: first, by reflection, which is noblest; second, by imitation, which is easiest; and third, by experience, which is the most bitter."—Confucius

Writing in a journal is one of the most effective ways to be reflective as well as capture your feelings, thoughts, and observations in a manner that is organized so that you may put them to good use in the future. For example, journaling can serve as an important and helpful tool for evaluating and improving your work by recording your professional growth over time. In addition to assisting with your professional development, writing down your thoughts and feelings on a regular basis can also help with stress management and be an integral part of your self-care routine.

Keeping a journal may also prove to be particularly useful if you are observing classrooms as part of your teacher preparation. With a journal, you can organize your impressions, the things that you notice, and general thoughts about these classroom observations. Below is a short list of questions that could be answered in your journal and a sample journal entry from a classroom observation.

SAMPLE GUIDING QUESTIONS

- What type of classroom did I observe (i.e., mainstream, resource, inclusive)?
- How is the classroom arranged and/or organized?
- What evidence supports that students were learning?
- What strategies does the teacher use to address the students' specific needs?

- Are the lessons collaboratively planned across disciplines?
- For special education, what support services were utilized?
- What were other impressions?

SAMPLE JOURNAL ENTRY

The first impression that I have from my observations was in a mainstream classroom with a general education teacher and a special education teacher. My overriding impression is that the special education teacher was not fully utilized. I was dismayed by the fact that the special education teacher and the general education teachers did not collaborate in their planning, despite the fact that they knew it was a best practice and, ultimately, would benefit all the students. For instance, I noted that one student with ADHD finished his work in nearly half the time than his classmates did. I cannot comment on how accurate his work was, but I do know that he began to act out once he became bored with having nothing to do. In using collaborative planning, the general education teacher and the special education teacher could have developed new and challenging classwork for when this student finished normal classwork earlier than the rest of the class. This potentially would improve the student's performance and behavior.

The biggest challenge of keeping a journal is carving out time to write on a regular and consistent basis. As it is such a critical tool in professional development, you should strive to make writing in your journal a habit. Here are a few suggestions to help you:

- Keep a spiral notebook and pen next to your bed. Before you go to sleep, unwind by unloading all your thoughts into your journal for about 10–15 minutes.
- Schedule daily writing time.
- Write directly after a class you have taken or taught.
- Create or join a weblog (blog) and post entries regularly. Then, read the advice and words of encouragement posted from other teachers reading your blog.

If you encounter writer's block, below are a few writing prompts:

- Outline any advice you have received.
- Summarize the day: What were the high and low points?
- Highlight ideas you could use in your future classroom.
- Declare your short- and long-term goals.
- Take note of how you or another teacher dealt with a difficult situation.
- Describe general impressions about other teachers and students.

By striving to include journal writing as part of your routine, you will continue the teaching process and, in a short time, will begin to see significant personal and professional growth. Ultimately, this growth will help you to create a better learning environment for your students as you continue to collect and use this information to build on your knowledge foundation.

Chapter 5

Organize for the edTPA™

"Spectacular achievement is always preceded by unspectacular preparation."—Robert H. Schuller

The Teacher Performance Assessment (edTPA™) was operationally launched in fall 2013 and, since then, has been widely used in teacher preparation. This performance-based assessment is designed to measure the classroom practice of teacher candidates. As part of the edTPA process, teacher candidates submit a portfolio that includes artifacts, video of their instruction—typically captured during student teaching—and a commentary that critically analyzes aspects of their practice: planning, instruction, and assessment. In turn, the edTPA submissions are evaluated against a set of scoring rubrics. The edTPA is now being used in more than 800 preparation programs in forty-one states and the District of Columbia (https://scale.stanford.edu/teaching/edtpa). In many states, as part of a statewide certification policy, passing the edTPA is consequential to receiving teacher licensure.

Because of the growing importance and consequential nature of the edTPA, teacher candidates would benefit from planning and organizing for this assessment early in their teacher preparation. Additional edTPA-specific strategies are offered in the student teaching section of this book. The overall strategies curated in this book stem from multiple sources: teacher candidates who have successfully completed the edTPA, edTPA assessors, university field supervisors, SCALE resources, and more. The edTPA strategies offered here are not exhaustive, yet will serve as another resource to guide you through the process and, hopefully, maximize the effort and success you have in completing the edTPA.

PREPARE WITH THE END IN MIND

Dr. Stephen Covey, the best-selling author of *The 7 Habits of Highly Effective People*, remarked, "To begin with the end in mind means to start with a clear understanding of your destination. It means to know where you are going so that you better understand where you are now and that the steps you take are always in the right direction."

This same advice is applicable when preparing yourself for the edTPA. Having the "end in mind" allows you to know the edTPA expectations. For example, by reviewing the edTPA expectations, you will begin to better understand what is required to score a 4 or 5 on any given scoring rubric. By preparing early on, you gain insight into your strengths and gaps in understanding related to the edTPA expectations. For instance, you may realize you do not know how to achieve a 4 or 5 on a specific rubric. That awareness will help you as you progress through the teacher training. You are more likely to make connections between your teacher preparation coursework and practicum to the edTPA—hopefully leveraging your strengths and closing those knowledge gaps so you will be more successful in completing the assessment.

To develop a "clear understanding," first, gather the necessary resources that provide the edTPA expectations. Generally, teacher candidates may access the resources via their teacher preparation program. The recommended resources are 1) the assessment handbook, 2) the Rubric Level Progressions booklet, and 3) the candidate support resource called *Making Good Choice*. Be sure to double-check that you have the correct handbook and that it is the latest edition.

Next, review all three resources as early as possible. If lack of time is an issue, start with the Understanding Rubric Level Progressions. This resource unpacks the expectations for each edTPA. One former teacher candidate commented, "Absolutely have the Rubric Level Progressions and use them religiously. You have to know where you're aiming."

It is further suggested that you take notes, writing down big takeaways and lingering questions. These notes will be a good way to keep yourself engaged as you read through the resources and will serve as a parking lot for questions that you will eventually want to be addressed. Also, revisit these resources throughout your training to track your growth toward meeting the edTPA expectations. Finally, later in the book, additional edTPA tips are provided to guide you through the planning, writing, and video-taping process while you are student teaching.

Chapter 6

Prioritize Self-Care

"Research-based educational strategies and pedagogy are only as good as the person providing them. And if the human providing the strategies is so depleted, worn out, and burned out that he or she can hardly breathe, then the expectation that he or she can provide oxygen to students in unrealistic. And yet this is what we are asking educators to do, day in and day out."—Tina Boogren

Developing awareness of self-care is an important step on your journey to becoming a teacher. Regardless of being a teacher candidate, student teacher, or job applicant, at some point (or regularly), you will be challenged both physically and mentally by the demands of this profession. Attention to self-care is paramount to ensure you are whole and healthy not only for your own personal well-being but also for your students and their families. Every child deserves an educator who is present, rested, positive, and passionate about the work. To start your self-care efforts, accept imperfection, set boundaries, build healthy habits, and continue learning.

DITCH PERFECTIONISM

Many teacher candidates identify themselves as perfectionists, and this can be a struggle. Think for a moment—do you identify as a perfectionist or have strong tendencies toward perfectionism? What are the drawbacks of perfectionism? How might we think about this differently? Dr. Brené Brown, researcher and best-selling author, offers this view on perfectionism from her book *The Gifts of Imperfection: Let Go of Who You Think You're Supposed to Be and Embrace Who You Are*:

Perfectionism is not the same thing has striving to be your best. Perfectionism is not about healthy achievement and growth. Perfectionism is the belief that if we live perfect, look perfect, and act perfect, we can minimize or avoid the pain of blame, judgment, and shame. It's a shield. Perfectionism is a twenty-ton shield that we lug around thinking it will protect us when, in fact, it's the thing that's really preventing us from flight (p. 56).

Perfectionism—this "twenty-ton shield that we lug around"—takes shape in different ways for teacher candidates. One way teacher candidates may be weighed down is in their pursuit of the perfect grade or grade point average. This aim for academic perfection may fuel an unhealthy pressure in teacher candidates, and this pressure can contribute to the teacher candidate valuing their grade above the learning. In addition, unhealthy expectations may also lead to poor health outcomes. For example, perfectionists pulling those all-nighters to get in that "perfect" paper may face the consequences of falling ill because of a worn-down immune system.

Perfectionism may also inhibit educators from taking healthy pedagogical risks to grow their practice. For instance, teacher candidates who are lesson planning or practicing a teaching method may hold back from trying a new strategy. Playing it safe may stem from a fear of feeling shame and judgment if the attempted new risk—an idea, change, technique, method—falls flat and does not have the desired effect. However, here is the reality: Teaching is messy and dynamic. As an educator, you must learn to be comfortable in this messiness. There is no such thing as the perfect teacher or the perfect lesson plan, so try to let go of that expectation early on and stop yourself from pretending that it exists.

All in all, one must learn to accept the imperfect by letting go of the unreasonable expectations of perfection and reach outside of one's comfort zone to take healthy risks. Have a zany idea to engage your students? Go for it. But, keep in mind, with imperfection comes plenty of failures, missteps, and mistakes. However, do not let that feeling of defeat overcome you, as it is in your failures that you will truly begin to grow as an educator. Own these failures, reflect upon them, and try again. Finally, work to be a role model for your students by showing that failing is healthy and often necessary in order to grow and learn.

SET BOUNDARIES

Strive to set healthy professional boundaries early on because you will quickly find that the demands are high in teacher preparation and the field of education, in general. To put it plainly, the work never stops. The sooner you realize and can accept this reality, the sooner you can take relief in pulling back and focusing on you. As a teacher candidate, there will always be a bit more you can do to improve or prepare for. As an educator, there will always be grading, lesson planning, answering emails, and other countless tasks to complete. The work of being a teacher can and will quickly overshadow your personal life if you are not mindful of setting boundaries. And it is because educators care so deeply about the students that they often allow the professional work to become all-consuming of their time, attention, and energy. Remember, though, while being a teacher is an integral part of your identity, it is not your full identity.

Setting healthy boundaries as an educator allows you to tend to the other important parts of your life: your family, friends, and interests/hobbies. Boundaries are personal and will look different for each person. For example, you may make it a rule not to check your work email after a certain time and limit working on the weekends. Creating these work boundaries will take a bit of experimenting to determine what works best for you. The most important part, though, is that you try something and then reflect on how it is working for you.

Next, communicate what these boundaries are to those who will be affected by them. For instance, you might tell your partner that you will not write or grade papers after a certain time—that's your cutoff. This sharing will help create some amount of accountability to adhering to your boundaries. Finally, give yourself grace if you don't fully live up to these guidelines you have set. The purpose is not perfection, but self-preservation, allowing you to tend to your whole self.

FORM HEALTHY HABITS

Next, consider incorporating one (or several) of the self-care habits below into your daily or weekly routine. Embracing and sticking to even one new habit can make a noticeable difference in your well-being. To help get you started, below are five useful self-care habits:

1. Drink plenty of water or tea. Try to drink a full glass of water right after waking up to immediately hydrate the body. Also, consider buying a cheap coffeemaker and bring it to your classroom. Throughout the day, you can enjoy one or two cups of green tea. You are likely to find your energy is so much greater because of this habit.
2. Get massages. Schedule massages regularly. Often with a medical doctor's referral for massage therapy, insurance will cover most of the expense. Check with your insurance provider about your coverage.

3. Practice gratitude. In the morning, build a routine of thinking of three unique things that you are grateful for each day. This habit will help shift you into a more positive mindset.
4. Take a nap. Consider carving out ten to twenty minutes a day to nap. Finding time to do so may be difficult, but consider your lunch break or right after school. Routinely napping can have a noticeable improvement to your physical and mental health. To learn more about the researched benefits of naps, read Daniel Pink's book *When: The Scientific Secrets of Perfect Timing*.
5. Go for a walk. Set a goal to walk at least three times a week. Walking gives you space to brainstorm, strategize, be present, or focus on thoughts of gratitude.

Here are other self-care habits to consider:

- Take nature walks: Walk slow, look for wildlife, and listen.
- Set a workout routine.
- Start a garden (or bring a plant to put on your desk at work!).
- Watch less TV.
- Make yourself a priority. Block out time on your schedule just for you.
- Meet an old friend for coffee or drinks.
- Start a journal. Set a timer for three minutes and write freely.
- Practice mindful breathing exercises.
- Wake up fifteen to thirty minutes before you must get up. These extra minutes will help ease you into your day.
- Take a long bath.
- Attend a comedy show with a friend.
- Channel your creative juices: Write or do art. If you need some inspiration, look for mindfulness magazines such as *Flow* and *Project Calm* at your local bookstore.
- Read for enjoyment.
- Practice intentionality. Focus on one task at a time.
- Visit local libraries and museums. Don't watch the clock; just let yourself wander and explore.

CONTINUE YOU

Finally, this book does not pretend to be a comprehensive self-care resource, but rather provides some insight by offering a few key strategies—be imperfect, set boundaries, and develop healthy habits—to start you on your journey of self-care. Therefore, it is incumbent on you to invest time in learning more about self-care and building healthy habits. To continue learning, become aware of the incredible people doing work in this area. To start, lean into social media. Social media offers community and resources around self-care, especially as self-care intersects with education. Search #selfcare on Twitter or Facebook to discover other educators, incredible ideas, and thought leaders on this important topic.

SUGGESTED READING

Tina Boogren, *Take Time for You: Self-Care Action Plans for Educators (Using Maslow's Hierarchy of Needs and Positive Psychology)* (Bloomington, Solution Tree Press, 2018).

Chapter 7

A Novice Teacher's Perspective

Growth Comes from Imperfection

Leann Schumacher

Throughout my entire first year of teaching, I often found myself struggling with perfectionism. It was a pervasive feeling that crept up every time I would leave my classroom and quickly became a familiar form of torture. My walk through the hallways always involved peering into others classrooms and thinking, "I wish I could get my reading corner that tidy!" or "Where does he find the time to keep everything *that* organized?" or "Wow, she is such a better teacher than I am." By the time I had made it back to my messy, disorganized classroom, I would feel utterly deflated.

Sadly, as a novice teacher, my story is not unique. New teachers often feel an insurmountable amount of pressure their first year to prove themselves to their colleagues, students, and administrators. When we inevitably start drowning in the classroom management, the curriculum, the emails, we look to more experienced teachers to "save us." We see the seemingly amazing job they are doing and try to emulate them, thinking our shortcomings will be solved if we do. However, time and time again we still fall short. These experienced teachers are like icebergs: All we notice is the beautifully crafted slice of perfection. Below the surface, in the dark parts we can't see, was that educators' long, arduous journey to get to that point: all of their failures, the trial-and-error efforts, and the hardships they had to face that contribute to where they are now today. So, those feelings of inadequacy, that feeling that you are doing it all wrong—it's all part of the process. Teaching is messy, and whether you are two months or twenty years in, it's never going to be perfect—ever. Embrace your imperfections because they are what make you a unique and invaluable educator.

Chapter 8

Differentiate Yourself Through Education

"The beautiful thing about learning is that no one can take it away from you."—B.B. King

Administrators are looking for teachers who are flexible, who are dedicated, and who will be an asset to their school and the community in more ways than one. In a competitive job market, you must seek ways to stand out from your peers—one great way is through education.

Imagine you are the hiring principal. You have an open high school social studies position, and you have narrowed the field to two highly qualified candidates:

- Candidate A is a recent graduate who interviewed well and is certified to teach social studies.
- Candidate B is also a recent graduate. She interviewed well and is certified to teach social studies and English language learners (also referred to as ELs—English learners).

Examining both of these highly qualified candidates, which one would you choose? The principal would hire candidate B. Candidate B is a greater asset to the school because she can teach social studies, provide stronger support for her English learners in the class, and, if necessary, teach ELL social studies classes. In short, she would be a fantastic resource, especially if the school's student demographics are trending toward an increase in English learners.

Evaluate your own situation. Which candidate would you typify: A or B? Take a moment and answer these questions:

- Are you specializing in a high-need area, such as special education, math, science, and/or EL?
- Are you a male seeking an elementary teaching position?
- Are you willing to relocate to teach in a hard-to-staff school (e.g., rural)?
- Have you done anything to set yourself apart from other job seekers?

If you cannot answer "yes" to at least one of these questions, consider taking additional professional education courses to improve your chances of being hired in the school or district of your choice, especially if this extra effort leads to becoming certified/endorsed in more than one teaching area. Not only will you broaden your educational credentials, but you will also become a more knowledgeable and well-rounded teacher. Additional endorsements will also show potential employers your drive and dedication to continued professional growth.

The added credentials also provide you with more options and opportunities throughout your teaching career. For example, after some years of teaching, you may decide you need a change. That additional certification will allow you to pursue new teaching opportunities, perhaps even within the same school. Another potential benefit is that the added coursework, endorsements, or certifications may increase your income by pushing you up in the pay schedule. Of course, this will differ from state to state and district to district.

Chapter 9

Become an Expert on a Particular Concept

"What's the use of running if you are not on the right road?"—German proverb

A clever way to differentiate yourself from your peers is by becoming an expert in one or a few areas. As you progress through your teacher preparation program, strive to organize your studies, whenever possible, around a central theme. When given an opportunity to choose a research topic, stick to one education topic of interest to you. Perhaps you have an interest in interdisciplinary teams, cooperative learning, racial equity, or special education. By building on a central theme throughout your academic career, you do the following:

- Become an expert on that topic, building on your knowledge with each class you take and teach.
- Reduce your workload, by using your research for more than one project.
- Build references and research that may be used later for a graduate degree.

In his best-selling business book *Good to Great*, Jim Collins (2001) identifies the concept of sticking to one theme, at which you become an expert, as a core element in high-performing organizations. Collins recommends developing your theme or area of concentration from your answers to these three questions:

1. What are you deeply passionate about?
2. What can you be the best at?
3. What drives your work?

Take time to reflect on these questions. You may even find it beneficial to inquire from a trusted individual from your network on what they perceive your passions are and what drives your work. Once you identify and begin researching a topic that interests you, remember to organize it in a manner that makes the most sense to you. It might be best to create a single folder to keep all your work and research together.

Chapter 10

Address Your Growth Areas

"To be idle is a short road to death and to be diligent is a way of life; foolish people are idle, wise people are diligent."—Buddha

Yet another way to continue differentiating yourself from other recent graduates is to demonstrate competency not only in your subject matter but also in your ability to apply and use effective pedagogy. Many teacher candidates who follow the traditional teacher education programs and complete their certification are strong in pedagogy but weaker in the subject matter, whereas someone entering into the teaching profession from their given industry or field of study may be stronger in the subject matter but weaker in pedagogy.

Use your preservice teaching experience to identify and strengthen your weak areas and to grow professionally. After school or during the summer, take advantage of any and all opportunities to gain further insight into your content area or to strengthen your pedagogy. Your efforts will pay off by creating meaningful work experiences that will differentiate you from other job seekers.

In summary, look for opportunities to excel and grow on those off days or during the summer. Below are a few ideas to kick-start your thinking on how to potentially deepen your content knowledge and strengthen your instructional skills.

EXAMPLES IN HOW TO BECOME MORE COMPETENT IN YOUR SUBJECT MATTER

- Volunteer in an organization that researches or supports your content area. For example, if you are an art teacher, you could volunteer at the local art

gallery or museum. You could then meet local artists who might later be helpful in your own classroom.
- Find an internship or a job in your content area.
- Attend a workshop or a course at the local community college.

EXAMPLES TO DEVELOP A STRONGER PEDAGOGY

- Substitute-teach in your local school system. This is a wonderful way to learn about teaching and the different schools in your community.
- Volunteer or work in student summer programs. Such programs as TRIO Upward Bound can be found in hundreds of communities across the United States.
- Tutor and mentor students. You can work with local private tutoring companies or advertise your own services.

Chapter 11

Benefit from Networking in Schools

"The currency of real networking is not greed but generosity."—Keith Ferrazzi

Networking plays a vital and necessary role in obtaining a teaching job. To network means to actively create and nourish connections and relationships with others. A healthy network includes mutual support of each other and a sharing of knowledge, skills, and, possibly, contacts. In this first section, specific strategies are presented to highlight ways to build a healthy network during your teacher preparation.

To start, having a presence in schools is a fantastic way to network. There are many ways to have a presence: becoming an employee (e.g., instructional aide, recess monitor, etc.), volunteering, or substitute-teaching. Successful networking hinges on you being actively engaged in nourishing your network. Understandably, networking does not come naturally to everyone. At times, joining a conversation can be tricky and small talk can seem trivial—overall, this can be emotionally draining. While networking can be difficult, this is not an excuse not to try. If you are frustrated with being outside the network of local teachers, channel your energy into breaking in and building your own network.

There are simple ways to start. To begin, immerse yourself with other teachers in the building. A great way to develop a presence is to mingle in the teachers' lounge and hallways. Next, join in on conversations with other teachers. Make the effort to introduce yourself to an unfamiliar face. One way to introduce yourself to someone new is by making an authentic compliment or inquiry. For example, you were impressed by how a teacher has her students transition. Introduce yourself, let the teacher know you appreciate how well the students transition, and ask her to unpack the strategy she uses to teach the transition. Not only will you have made a connection, but you will also have gained a new procedure to try in your own teaching.

Another way to build your network is by fostering a strong reputation. For example, if you substitute, provide superb, detailed class notes for the teacher, including accurate attendance records and names of students who were helpful and those who were challenging. Don't think that by talking about something that went wrong in the classroom, the regular teacher will think of you as incompetent and not call you back. On the contrary, teachers want to know exactly what happened while they were away to make sure the students are behaving to their expectations. Finally, leave your contact information (name, phone number, email address, and/or your substitute teacher ID number, if you have one), so they can request you again. Consider creating simple business cards and leaving a few each time you volunteer or substitute-teach. Generally, with a strong reputation, other teachers will talk about you and recommend you, further getting your name out there.

In the end, know that networking may be awkward and you may stumble. Give yourself grace as you build your networking skills. Eventually, with some patience and tenacity, you will see the fruits of your labor as your confidence and ability in dealing with people begins to grow.

Chapter 12

Get Face Time with Administrators

"Facing it, always facing it, that's the way to get through. Face it."
—Joseph Conrad

Expanding your network to include administrators (principals, vice principals, deans, etc.) will be a benefit that pays dividends once you begin your job search. It may seem daunting at first, but making these connections early on will give you a leg up if you wish to teach at a particular school or district. If you are substitute-teaching, visiting, volunteering, or observing, make it a point to have face time with administrators as often as possible, without, of course, being a nuisance.

While most administrators may not remember you by name, in an interview they will recall your friendly face as having some context with their school. This alone can give you an advantage over other faceless job applicants administrators have to choose from. With stronger connections, the administrator may also clue you in to employment opportunities within their school by encouraging you to apply, putting in a good word for you with human resources, or even making you an offer. The administrator may also recommend you to other principals who are in need of teaching staff if they do not have a position available for you at their school.

Again, strive to become a familiar face in the school building. Greet administrators in the hallways as they hustle back and forth between classrooms. Meet them in casual settings, such as the school lunchroom or recess playground, or when the administrator is not putting out the proverbial fire. Also, if assisting a classroom teacher, consider volunteering to make visits to the office to pick up such things as mail or supplies as a way to increase your presence and opportunities for interactions.

Chapter 13

Network within Your Teacher Education Program

"A teacher affects eternity; he can never tell where his influence stops."
—Henry Adams

Your professors and peers within your teacher preparation program can provide another rich opportunity for networking. Together, these two groups encompass diverse experiences and backgrounds that may be of great benefit to you as you embark on your teaching career. Take as an example your peers as a network. As you progress through your teacher education program, you and your peers may send timely communication to each other about upcoming job openings in your respective schools or districts. Your peers may even put in a good word for you with the administration, possibly giving you an advantage over others applying.

Additionally, your professors and instructors represent a wealth of knowledge and therefore can also be a valuable asset to your network. Keep in mind that many of your instructors, as former teachers or administrators, may be willing to share pertinent information with you to assist in my job search. For instance, faculty may also provide insight into the job market, such as which schools/districts are hiring, as well as guidance on what principals are looking for in potential job candidates. This information may give a teacher candidate the critical edge needed to land the job they desire. Lastly, faculty can provide you with constructive feedback on how to improve your cover letter and résumé, as well as write you a letter of recommendation or serve as a job reference.

Chapter 14

Consider Everyone Part of Your Network

"Invisible threads make the strongest ties."—Friedrich Nietzche

Networks are fluid and dynamic, and a well-built one should be all-encompassing. Therefore, it is wise to look for possible connections beyond the teachers and administrators with whom you may normally interact. Consider if any of your family, neighbors, friends, or former colleagues have connections to education. For instance, your neighbor might be a former principal with close to ties the school community or your best friend's mother might be a teacher. Push outside of your circle of friends and colleagues for possible connections. Include in your thinking people from all areas of your life: clubs, civic organizations, religious places, etc.

After brainstorming, make a list of anyone that comes to mind and note how he or she is connected to education. This is a critical building block in establishing your network. By listing people whom you may have strong or weak connections to, you are increasing the likelihood of getting the teaching job you want. Take the example of the classic study *Getting a Job* by the sociologist Mark Gravovetter. In this study, Gravovetter concluded that 56 percent of people found a job through a personal connection. Only 20 percent of the study subjects found their jobs by applying directly to prospective employers. From this study, it appears more likely that you will find a job from someone whom you occasionally see, than by applying directly to a school. In short, consider anyone a possible contact, and by building these contacts, you, a future job candidate, will improve your chances of identifying that individual who may lead you to your desired job.

Chapter 15

Organize Your Contacts

"If you can organize your kitchen, you can organize your life."—Louis Parrish

As you build your network, it is a superb idea to begin assembling some type of organizational system for tracking your contact information. There are many approaches to managing your contacts; however, the key is to find an organizational system that is easy for you to manage and update on a regular basis. Maintaining a contact list can quickly become a burden if you choose a format that is time-consuming or not easily accessible. For this reason, it is wise to think carefully about what kind of system will work best for you and your needs before you begin.

Consider utilizing a web-based application to manage your network. You can create contact lists through free email accounts offered by Google or Microsoft. Using these services will allow you to easily create contacts and personalize with information such as shared interests, dates/places of meetings, mutual acquaintances, etc., for each related contact. Additionally, you will be able to share and retrieve information from any device with an Internet connection.

Further leverage your growing network by joining a professional networking site, such as LinkedIn (https://linkedin.com), which can also be accessed via an app. Simply import your email contacts, and you will be able to view their profiles, which will provide you with insight into their education, work experience, and interests. The site will also suggest new connections for you based on the contacts, groups, and organizations you choose to follow, providing even more opportunities for networking. LinkedIn offers other features as well, such as convenient messaging and the ability to join professional groups.

Table 15.1 Sample Format of a Contact List Using a Spreadsheet

Name	Title	Organization	Address	Phone	Email	Notes
Stacie Doe	Principal	Seattle High	123 Seattle High Ave.	206-555-5403	Stacie.Doe@seattle.edu	Met 5/5/18 at Seattle Career Fair. Told me of a possible job opening in the fall. Follow up in July.

Alternatively, you could store all your contacts in a spreadsheet, like Google Sheets or Microsoft Excel. This allows you to use special functions like sorting. See table 15.1 as an example of how to organize your contacts using a spreadsheet. And, if you wish, you can export your spreadsheet contact file into an email-contact platform or LinkedIn.

Finally, once you have established your organization system, stay actively engaged with your network by keeping in touch and sending updates on a regular basis. For instance, simply send an email (or use LinkedIn messaging) once every few months to say hello, tell them about changes in your life, and genuinely inquire about their lives as well. This concerted effort to keep in contact on a consistent basis will nurture stronger relationships. Networking is intended to be mutually beneficial for all parties involved; therefore, being proactive about regularly staying in touch will also keep you from being perceived as a person who reaches out only when they need something.

Section II

EXCEL AT STUDENT TEACHING

Chapter 16

Develop Your Philosophy and Core Values

"The philosophy of the schoolroom in one generation will be the philosophy of government in the next."—Abraham Lincoln

In this section of the book, you will learn strategies that will prepare you for student teaching. Student teaching is typically the culminating practicum experience where you apply what you have learned from your teacher training to a real classroom. A wise first step to prepare for student teaching is by developing a sound personal philosophy of education. The above quote from Abraham Lincoln illustrates the importance of your education philosophy, as it affects future generations and shapes society.

WHAT IS AN EDUCATION PHILOSOPHY STATEMENT?

An education philosophy statement is the bedrock of any master teacher; it encapsulates the principles and beliefs you bring to your teaching and creates the foundation and framework from which your classroom decisions are made. Once established, your philosophy will fundamentally remain the same but will evolve over time to reflect your teaching and life experiences and ongoing professional development. Since it is your foundation, it is important to have clarity of your education philosophy before you begin your journey in teaching.

WRITING AN EDUCATION PHILOSOPHY STATEMENT

Crafting a philosophy statement takes considerable time and reflection. To begin, reflect on the following questions and write your responses, perhaps using these questions as writing prompts for your journal:

- What motivated you to go into teaching?
- What values and beliefs would an ideal teacher have?
- What are your beliefs about students, learning, behavior, respect, schools, and general education?
- What changes would you like to see in our education system?
- What values do you want to model for the students inside and outside the classroom?
- Of your stated beliefs, which ones are nonnegotiable?

When you begin writing your education philosophy statement, remember that it is about you and your beliefs. Avoid writing educational buzzwords and phrases just to make it sound better. The best way to start is with "I believe..." Keep it short—no longer than one page of single-spaced type.

For illustrative purposes, below are two sample education philosophy statements from teacher candidates at the Ohio State University College of Education. As you read through these philosophy statements, notice how the formatting and approach express each writer's individuality. Although very different, both are effective and well-written. To be clear, it takes effort and time to write a concise, effective statement of philosophy, so do not give up on your first try. Continue to revisit your philosophy statement and, periodically, reflect on the ways in which this living document reflects your core beliefs and pedagogical practices.

Example 1 of an Education Philosophy Statement

I believe the children are our future...

I believe each and every child has the potential to bring something unique and special to the world. I will help children to develop their potential by believing in them as capable individuals. I will assist children in discovering who they are, so they can express their own opinions and nurture their own ideas. I have a vision of a world where people learn to respect, accept, and embrace the differences between us, as the core of what makes life so fascinating.

Teach them well and let them lead the way...

Every classroom presents a unique community of learners that varies not only in abilities, but also in learning styles. My role as a teacher is to give children the tools with which to cultivate their own gardens of knowledge. To accomplish this goal, I will teach to the needs of each child so that all learners can feel capable and successful. I will present a curriculum that involves the interests of the children and makes learning relevant to life. I will incorporate themes, integrated units, projects, group work, individual work, and hands-on learning in order to make children active learners. Finally, I will tie learning into the world community to help children become caring and active members of society. Show them all the beauty they possess inside.

Give them a sense of pride...

My classroom will be a caring, safe, and equitable environment where each child can blossom and grow. I will allow children to become responsible members of our classroom community by using strategies such as class meetings, positive discipline, and democratic principles. In showing children how to become responsible for themselves as well as their own learning, I am giving them the tools to become successful in life, to believe in themselves, and to love themselves.

Let the children's laughter remind us how we used to be...

Teaching is a lifelong learning process of learning about new philosophies and new strategies, learning from the parents and community, learning from colleagues, and especially learning from the children. Children have taught me to open my mind and my heart to the joys, the innocence, and the diversity of ideas in the world. Because of this, I will never forget how to smile with the new, cherish the old, and laugh with the children.

Example 2 of an Education Philosophy Statement

I believe that each child is a unique individual who needs a secure, caring, and stimulating atmosphere in which to grow and mature emotionally, intellectually, physically, and socially. It is my desire as an educator to help students meet their fullest potential in these areas by providing an environment that is safe, supports risk-taking, and invites a sharing of ideas. There are three elements that I believe are conducive to establishing such an environment, (1) the teacher acting as a guide, (2) allowing the child's natural curiosity to direct his/her learning, and (3) promoting respect for all things and all people.

When the teacher's role is to guide, providing access to information rather than acting as the primary source of information, the students' search for knowledge is met as they learn to find answers to their questions. For students to construct knowledge, they need the opportunity to discover for themselves and practice skills in authentic situations. Providing students access to hands-on activities and allowing adequate time and space to use materials that reinforce the lesson being studied creates an opportunity for individual discovery and construction of knowledge to occur.

Equally important to self-discovery is having the opportunity to study things that are meaningful and relevant to one's life and interests. Developing a curriculum around student interests fosters intrinsic motivation and stimulates the passion to learn. One way to take learning in a direction relevant to student interest is to invite student dialogue about the lessons and units of study. Given the opportunity for input, students generate ideas and set goals that make for much richer activities than I could have created or imagined myself. When students have ownership in the curriculum, they are motivated to work hard and master the skills necessary to reach their goals.

Helping students to develop a deep love and respect for themselves, others, and their environment occurs through an open sharing of ideas and a judicious approach to discipline. When the voice of each student is heard, and environment evolves where students feel free to express themselves. Class meetings are one way to encourage such dialogue. I believe children have greater respect for their teachers, their peers, and the lessons presented when they feel safe and sure of what is expected of them. In setting fair and consistent rules initially and stating the importance of every activity, students are shown respect for their presence and time. In turn, they learn to respect themselves, others, and their environment.

For myself, teaching provides an opportunity for continual learning and growth. One of my hopes as an educator is to instill a love of learning in my students, as I share my own passion for learning with them. I feel there is a need for compassionate, strong, and dedicated individuals who are excited about working with children. In our competitive society, it is important for students to not only receive a solid education but to work with someone who is aware of and sensitive to their individual needs. I am such a person and will always strive to be the best educator that I can be.

Chapter 17

Proclaim Your Student Teaching Goals

"When we are motivated by goals that have deep meaning, by dreams that need completion, by pure love that needs expressing, then we truly live."—Greg Anderson

Student teaching is where the rubber meets the road. After years spent studying, practicing, and revising your pedagogy, it is now time to put it all to the test. However, as you begin, you may wonder to yourself, "How will I know if I am successful at student teaching?" A simple and practical way to measure this is by setting clear and quantifiable goals before you begin, monitoring your progress throughout your practicum, and celebrating your growth. Alternatively, entering this experience without a clear vision of where you are headed will potentially leave you, as one teacher candidate described it, "blindly muddling through student teaching." Therefore, it is wise to think carefully about what you want to gain from this culminating experience before you step foot into the classroom.

Refer back to the educational process of building a foundation of knowledge, applying that knowledge to teaching, and reflecting on how to improve. Goal setting is at the heart of this ongoing process of learning and professional growth. Every teacher (and student teacher) should be continually identifying areas in need of improvement to maintain a high level of efficacy in the classroom. The process is straightforward and cyclical: Set specific goals to meet that area of growth, work passionately to meet those goals, measure the results, and then begin again with another area in need of improvement. This process of goal setting, action, and evaluation should be evident in the educator's work, from lesson planning to professional development plans.

HOW TO SET EFFECTIVE GOALS

To begin setting your goals, first set aside time to review your education philosophy statement. Again, this philosophy statement should encompass your vision on how you will support your students and their learning, and on how you will manage your classroom. By extension, your student teaching goals should align with your philosophy. To illustrate this point, referring back to the previous sample philosophy statement, the Ohio State teacher candidate wrote:

> My role as a teacher is to give children the tools with which to cultivate their own gardens of knowledge. To accomplish this goal, I will teach to the needs of each child so that all learners can feel capable and successful. I will present a curriculum that involves the interests of the children and makes learning relevant to life. I will incorporate themes, integrated units, projects, group work, individual work, and hands-on learning in order to make children active learners.

Examining this part of her philosophy, a potential supportive goal could be to boost student engagement. More specifically, the teacher could set a goal of implementing a hands-on, multidisciplinary unit that is based on the students' interests during student teaching.

PROCLAIM YOUR GOALS

We all need encouragement and gentle reminders of what we are working toward. First, write down your goals (aim for two to three) and describe how you will measure them. Second, post your goals where you will see them every day—inside your visor in your car, on your nightstand, or taped to a mirror. In this way, you get a daily reminder of your goals. Moreover, it is extremely refreshing to cross off goals from your list as you accomplish them. Over time, you will be proud to see all that you have achieved. Last, but not least, communicate your goals to someone else. This person could be your cooperating teacher, your university supervisor, or a mentor. By putting your goals into the public domain, you are holding yourself accountable and you are more likely to follow up and meet those goals.

EVALUATE YOUR EFFECTIVENESS

Once you set goals that are measurable, that are challenging, that are attainable, and that support your philosophy, monitor and evaluate your progress in meeting those goals. Monitoring encompasses various qualitative and quantitative measures, such as observations, surveys, student work, testing, and performance evaluations. Take the earlier example and imagine you are working toward the aforementioned goal of increasing student engagement. You formatively assess student engagement by having students regularly self-report engagement levels on exit slips. You further use observations and one-on-one conferences to assess the level of student engagement. With ongoing monitoring, you can assess the results and continue to adjust your teaching until you have reached the established goal.

CELEBRATE YOUR GROWTH

As you diligently work toward your goals, keep in mind the brain's natural tendency toward a negativity bias. It is human nature to focus more on all of the bad that happens to us while completely ignoring the good. Teachers can be especially susceptible to this mindset as each day in the classroom can bring on a new set of challenges that will continually test their beliefs about their strengths and abilities. Therefore, for each goal you accomplish, take a moment to appreciate all of the hard work it took to get there. Give yourself time to relax, reflect, and celebrate each accomplishment. This practice of taking time to celebrate growth is an important part of self-care as it helps minimize your risk of burning out.

Chapter 18

Research the Community, School, and Students

"What is research but a blind date with knowledge?"—Will Harvey

An essential step in student teaching preparation is to do preliminary research to learn about your new school, its students, and the community. Chances are that you have never been in the school, nor have you met any of the students. If you are fortunate enough to student teach in a school that you are familiar with, either through work experience or visitation, then you are already ahead of the game. However, this is most often not the case, and the more background knowledge you have going in, the less your first day in the classroom will feel like a blind date.

LEARN ABOUT THE STUDENTS AND SCHOOL

To begin, make efforts to familiarize yourself with the students and their backgrounds, the school and its goals, and the climate of the school. Here are some possible ideas to get you started:

- Introduce yourself to students and their families by sending out a personalized introduction letter. Include some personal and professional information, as well as your education background and school contact information.
- Reach out to some of the school's current and former educators to gain some insiders' perspective.
- Be on the lookout for articles and news stories from the local media about the school or the district.
- Utilize social media (such as Twitter) by following the school's teachers or administrators (only if the accounts are professionally focused).

- Create Google Alerts—free email updates of the latest relevant Google results (web, news, etc.) based on your choice of a query.
- Participate in schoolwide events that involve the community, such as engineering night, concerts, or other similar events.

Additional insightful information may be gleaned by visiting your school, district, and state education websites. As you browse the sites, below are some questions to guide your research:

- What is the student makeup of the school (special education, bilingual, ethnic backgrounds, income)?
- What types of learning initiatives are in place at the school?
- What are the school's test scores? How are those scores trending? What are the areas of strength and areas of improvement?
- What is the typical class size?
- How many students and teachers are there?
- What kind of curricula and programs does the school offer?
- What makes that school or school district unique?

DEVELOP COMMUNITY AWARENESS

Schooling occurs in a social context and is part of a broader community. Thoroughly investigate the community, specifically looking for the community assets—the places and resources within the community that add value or improve the quality of life for the people.

Here are some ideas to develop community awareness:

- Read the local newspapers, especially the education section, to familiarize yourself with the community.
- Collect information about the school's neighborhood by reading up on things such as demographics, cost of living, and quality of life. In large cities or districts, neighborhoods can vary greatly from each other, causing a single school to represent a wide range of socioeconomic backgrounds. An easy way to uncover this specific information is to use Realtor Internet tools (e.g., Zillow).
- Take walks around the neighborhood.
- Dine in the local restaurants and enjoy the local coffee shops. Ask parents, students, and colleagues for suggestions.
- Visit the local cultural treasures such as museums, parks, farmers' markets, or other community gathering spaces.

- Participate in events happening around the community.
- Support the local economy (and business owners) by shopping in the neighborhood stores.

As a final note, when out and about in the community, take the time to engage with people in a meaningful way. Genuinely inquire and take an inventory about the things they love and appreciate about their local culture, community, and neighborhoods. You learn more about the area you will be teaching in, and you will begin to feel a sense of ownership and belonging during your practicum as you build strong ties and relationships with families.

Chapter 19

Keep Abreast of Your Field

"We now accept the fact that learning is a lifelong process of keeping abreast of change. And the most pressing task is to teach people how to learn."—Peter F. Drucker

To further prepare for student teaching and, as part of being a lifelong learner, you should be aware of the latest best practices in research. You can keep abreast of changes by joining general education and content-specific organizations and by reviewing educational journals and websites. These resources can provide you with curriculum ideas, connections to experts, publications, conferences, e-workshops, and job banks.

RESOURCES AND ORGANIZATIONS

Keep up to date on the latest education news and trends by reading *Education Week* (https://www.edweek.org)—a print and online newspaper that covers K–12 education. *Education Week* further offers a free job search service. Check with your school's library to see if they might have an institutional license, which could give you free access. Consider joining Phi Delta Kappa (PDK) (https://www.pdkintl.org). PDK is one of the premier education organizations. It publishes the *Kappan*—a practitioner-focused journal. The *Kappan* features articles about educational research, practice, and policy, as well as blogs and columns on school and district leadership, media coverage of education, legal issues in the field, state and federal politics, and more. PDK also has hundreds of local chapters, mostly on college campuses, which provides wonderful opportunities to network. Other benefits include scholarships and conferences focused on the preservice teacher.

Table 19.1 Professional Organizations by Concentration

Area of Concentration	Name of Professional Organization
Art	National Art Education Association
Bilingual	National Association for Bilingual Education
Business	Association for Career and Technical Education
Early Childhood	National Association for the Education of Young Children
Economics	Council for Economic Education
English/Language Arts	National Council of Teachers of English
Foreign Languages	American Council on the Teaching of Foreign Languages
Geography	National Council for Geographic Education
Health	American Association for Health Education
Information Technology	Association for the Advancement of Computing in Education
Library	American Library Association
Literacy	International Literacy Association
Math	National Council of Teachers of Mathematics
Middle School	Association for Middle Level Education
Music	Music Teachers National Association
Physical Education	National Association for Sports and Physical Education
Science	National Science Teachers Association
Social Studies	National Council for the Social Studies
Special Education: Exceptional Children	Council for Exceptional Children
Special Education: Gifted Children	American Association for Gifted Children
Technology	International Society for Technology in Education

Another practice to stay current is by locating research online. Education Resources Information Center (ERIC), supported by the Department of Education, is the world's premier database of journal and non-journal education literature, with nearly 1.2 million citations dating back to 1966. This site also provides access to full-text materials at no charge. ERIC's website is https://www.eric.ed.gov/. This is an ideal place to begin research on almost any education topic. Another recommended site is Google Scholar. Use these web resources as a springboard to implement research-based practices in your own classroom to improve student learning.

In table 19.1 educational organizations are listed that focus on specific content areas. Find your area of concentration and visit the organization's website to explore their teacher resources and tools.

Chapter 20

Communicate Early with Your Cooperating Teacher

"A smile is the universal welcome."—Max Eastman

There is no reason to wait until your first day of student teaching to begin building relationships with your cooperating teacher and students. Once you have received your student teaching placement, obtain the contact information for your cooperating teacher and call or email to set up an informal meeting and observation. Depending on your teacher preparation program, you will be spending anywhere between three to nine months in the classroom for your culminating practicum, and building quality rapport takes time. Therefore, being proactive about getting acquainted early on is a big step toward a positive and successful student teaching experience.

Below are helpful tips for the first meeting with your cooperating teacher and observing the classroom:

- Dress professionally, as first impressions always count. Keep in mind you are not only meeting your mentor teacher and students, but you are also introducing yourself as a new face in the school. It is usually better to be a little overdressed than underdressed. For men, a nice dress shirt with a tie and dress slacks would be appropriate. For women, a nice blouse with dress slacks or skirt would work nicely.
- Be ready for introductions. The teacher will most likely introduce you to the class during your visit, as students will be curious about who you are and why you are there. The cooperating teacher may also ask you to tell the class a little about yourself. To alleviate the stress of being put on the spot, prepare a brief twenty- to thirty-second introduction of yourself. Take time to practice your delivery before you head off to your meeting.

- Closely observe the teacher and classroom environment, being sure to take notes for future reference. Is there anything that strikes you about the instruction or the classroom itself? Write down any questions or thoughts that occur to you while observing.
- Smile and interact with the class as much as possible. Avoid being the proverbial fly on the wall, and spend time meeting and talking with students to begin establishing a rapport. However, be mindful of the cooperating teacher to avoid being a distraction during instruction. A great time to approach students is when they are doing individual or group work, as you can engage them on both a personal and academic level.
- Develop a sense of what the students have learned and what they are currently learning by taking time to talk with the cooperating teacher and gather some resources. Ask about what they are studying right now and what units are coming up next. Inquire if there is a pacing guide or curriculum map you could review to get a better sense of the scope and sequence for the grade level or subject matter you will be teaching. If the students routinely use a classroom textbook, ask to borrow a spare one. Any and all information you can gather will serve as a jumping-off point for your lesson planning. In addition, you can begin to identify potential lesson segments that could be used for completing your edTPA.
- Ensure lines of communication stay open by asking the cooperating teacher the best way to contact him or her with further questions or to request feedback on lesson plans. In addition, don't be afraid to share your student teaching goals and even some of your worries. Remember that your cooperating teacher was once a student teacher preparing for the first day in the classroom.
- Express your sincere enthusiasm and gratitude about getting to learn and work side by side with the cooperating teacher and his or her students. This teacher is not only serving as your mentor, but they are also opening up their classroom and entrusting you with the learning and growth of their students. Everybody loves a little praise, so show you genuinely care by complimenting the cooperating teacher on something you observed. Whether it is the setup of the classroom, the behavior of the students, or an instructional strategy used, they will appreciate that you noticed their hard work and attention to detail.

Finally, if you are taking the edTPA, communication with your cooperating teacher is crucial. In some cases, your cooperating teacher may not be aware of the edTPA. Therefore, it's important to communicate early with your cooperating (mentor) teacher about the edTPA, its expectations, and your initial implementation plan. Your cooperating teacher may serve as a useful ally in helping you navigate the edTPA process because they are intimately familiar with the students (their strengths and learning needs). The cooperating teacher may also advise you in your lesson planning, such as figuring out the most effective ways to differentiate your instruction and assessment based on students' needs, and determining ways to include student voice.

Chapter 21

Working with Your Cooperating Teacher

"There is no such thing as a self-made man. You will reach your goals only with the help of others."—George Shinn

In education, as with any field, you will find yourself working side by side with people from a variety of backgrounds, with personalities and approaches that will differ from your own. Student teaching will be no exception. Since you will be under the tutelage of your mentor (cooperating) teacher, you will be required to work closely and professionally with him or her throughout your practicum. However, teacher candidates may run into problems if the cooperating teacher they are paired up with is a bad fit.

Depending on your preparation program, you may not have much say in the student teaching placement, as teacher education programs often determine the placement for you and will usually take into consideration only your preferences of district and grade level. Therefore, your choice of cooperating teacher is oftentimes completely out of your control. You may be partnered with a teacher who is supportive and open to new ideas and approaches, or, on the other side of the spectrum, you may be paired with a teacher who is inflexible and unsupportive.

A common "bad" experience in student teaching may begin with a controlling cooperating teacher who demands, if not requires, that a certain curriculum is covered and delivered in a prescribed way. Such cooperating teachers may seem to be trying to create carbon copies of themselves, but, under these conditions, they only manage to stifle the creativity of the student teacher. Alternatively, you may have a cooperating teacher who is not structured, is more free-flowing, and seems to create lesson plans while driving to work. This loose framework can cause problems because the student teacher is struggling to get their hands on something concrete (such as a curriculum) that they can work from. If either of these cases happens to you, do not despair; there are proactive steps you can take to keep your practicum on track.

First, approach the situation with a positive and forward-looking attitude. As much as you may feel frustrated by your placement, or feel that it is unfair, giving in to those negative feelings will only make matters worse. Keep in mind that the real reason you are there is to teach. Your students deserve a teacher who is happy and excited to see them, and who is fully invested in their continued growth. Learning to set aside the negative feelings and "leave them at the door" is a critical skill that will be crucial throughout your entire teaching career.

Second, despite how you may be feeling, continue working toward building a positive relationship with the cooperating teacher. Although the situation may be delicate, it is important for you to regularly communicate some of the ideas you would like to try. If the cooperating teacher does not take to any of your ideas, solicit their advice on what modifications can be made in order for it to work in their classroom. A majority of the time, this buy-in approach will work, as it shows the cooperating teacher that you respect their teaching style and learning environment.

In the end, if all else fails, remember the old adage oft repeated in education: "It is easier to ask for forgiveness than permission." However, do not do anything so drastic that it would jeopardize your relationship with the cooperating teacher or risk your final grade for student teaching. Ultimately, while student teaching is an important step, it is still just one part of your journey to becoming a teacher. No matter how tough it is, keep in mind that you have to work with this teacher for only a short and finite amount of time, and it will be over sooner than you realize. In a short time, you will have your own classroom, where you can freely implement your pedagogical and curriculum ideas.

Chapter 22

A Cooperating Teacher's Perspective

Advice for Student Teachers

Leah Krippner, a Cooperating Teacher

Consider the entire student teaching experience as an extended job interview: Dress professionally, camouflage piercings and tattoos, and avoid sharing anecdotes of having been fired from a job or of substance-involved antics. Similarly, remember that it is acceptable to be friendly with students but not to be their friends. Resist the urge to share personal stories not related to curriculum, particularly if you teach at the secondary level. Come to work on time and don't cut out early. Be the ideal employee the school is looking to hire.

Listen more than you speak. It is typically the hallmark of new teachers to go on and on about how they have been anointed as classroom deities and how they can hardly believe classrooms functioned before they set foot in one. It is great to think this; just keep it to yourself. If you listen to the experienced voices around you, you may pick up some great tips.

Find amiable colleagues and eat lunch with them every day no matter how busy you are. It is healthy to be chummy with teachers other than just the one to which you are officially assigned.

Keep the main office (administration) happy. Turn in attendance and grades in a timely manner. Answer parent phone calls promptly.

Grade in the same manner as your cooperating teacher does. You can develop your own style later. Remember that your cooperating teacher will have to seamlessly take over again.

Visit other classrooms. Observe for alternate teaching and disciplinary styles as well as variances in the organization (do they have bins, mailboxes, file folders, binders, etc.?). Mentally file these observations for when you need to try something new.

It is okay to use the preservice experience to decide that teaching is not for you. Very few education candidates have any real insight into the actual day-to-day rigors of classroom teaching. For most of us, our only previous exposure is watching our own teachers, which fails to shed light on issues like strife between colleagues, tedium, administrative hassles, workload, hostile parents, and evaluation. Of course, it is also okay to discover what you love about teaching during this time.

Chapter 23

Tackling the edTPA

"We think, mistakenly, that success is the result of the amount of time we put in at work instead of the quality of time we put in."—Ariana Huffington

Preparation is key to tackling any new endeavor—the edTPA is no exception. Take into consideration the following strategies to put you on more solid footing before you jump into lesson planning and videotaping for the edTPA.

KNOW YOUR STUDENTS

Accomplished teachers continuously learn about their students and, in turn, use this knowledge to inform their planning, instruction, and assessment. A core proposition of the National Board of Professional Teaching Standards reads, "[Teachers] treat students equitably, recognizing the individual differences that distinguish one student from another and taking account of these differences in their practice. They adjust their practice based on observation and knowledge of their students' interests, abilities, skills..." etc. The edTPA's expectations are no different. Regarding Planning Task 1, the edTPA *Making Good Choices* handbook stresses that you "demonstrate your depth of knowledge of your students in relation to the learning segment you plan to teach" and that "surface-level connections" are insufficient (2018, p. 12).

As soon as you learn of your placement (the class in which you will be doing your edTPA), begin investigating and writing about your students: the class demographics, significant subgroups of students with similar characteristics, students' varied strengths (including personal, cultural, and community assets), language development, and learning needs. Remember to review the Context for Learning expectations. As you begin learning more about the students and their community, consider how you will leverage their strengths and assets to assist them in meeting their learning targets. For instance, perhaps there is a respected community member with whom you could collaborate to enhance the classroom-to-community connections, thus increasing the authenticity and impact of the lessons.

To learn about your students and the community, refer back to the earlier strategy *Research the Community, School, and Students*. To briefly recap, immerse yourself in the community and observe the spaces to which students naturally gravitate. Next, gather additional information by being inquisitive. Finally, create a list of local community resources and organizations that could be considered community assets.

PREPARING FOR VIDEOTAPING

In the process of researching edTPA strategies for this book, a majority of the teacher candidates interviewed discussed the importance of preparing for videotaping. To start, be proactive by sending out your videotaping permission forms as soon as possible to families. Getting your permission forms out to families early on allows for ample time (hopefully) for you to follow up with any families that have not returned the permission slips. It is wise to anticipate that a few students will not grant permission or return the form to you. If you find yourself in this situation, just be sure that the students' faces and names do not appear in the video.

Next, consider how you will videotape your interactions, in particular, determining what equipment you will use and where you will place your videotaping device. It is also recommended to set up the camera and have a few trial runs before taping for your learning segment. Conducting some practice runs with the camera can be beneficial for a few reasons. One, you can determine if the placement of the camera will work for your specific needs, such as capturing only the students who have turned in their permission forms. A secondary benefit is that because students all initially react differently with cameras in the classroom, a few trial runs will give them a chance to adjust to being recorded and having the camera rolling while you are teaching. One teacher candidate described her experience videotaping for her edTPA: "I had lots of kids being sneaky with funny faces." In short, set clear expectations for the students, and emphasize why you are videotaping: to reflect on your teaching and to improve. You may also want to underscore to the students that you will be reviewing each recording.

Chapter 24

A University Field Supervisor's Perspective

edTPA Tips from the Field

Judy Longstreth, University Field Supervisor

Over the past six years that I have been working with the edTPA, I have come to realize that there are several mistakes that teacher candidates make when they begin writing for the edTPA. This is a quick guide to help avoid common mistakes and improve your success with this huge project.

- Read your whole handbook.
- Pay particular attention to what is needed for videotaping, academic language and language function, and reflections.
- Review the *Understanding Rubric Level Progressions* booklet on what is needed to get a score of 3 and 4 on each rubric.

Next, begin to prepare for writing the lesson plans with all your notes in hand. Consider the following questions in your lesson planning:

- What curriculum mini-unit will you teach over three to five days?
- What days will you teach the mini-unit?
- Which days on the calendar will you film? Who will film your videos? Or are you going to simply set up an iPad to record yourself?
- What kind of supports will you need to make or have available for your students to use? What research will you be using to support your instructional strategies? Attempt to find eight to ten pieces of research to back up your instructional strategies.
- In which lesson(s) will you cover academic language and your chosen language function? Where will the students be able to use the supports?

- Map out each video so you get exactly what you want on the video within the time limit. See the Evidence Chart for the time limits.
- Film additional videos (two or more) on different days so that you can select the best one to submit to be scored. Additionally, if you don't pass the assessment, you have extra film for the rewrite.
- Be intentional about identifying students who will need accommodations in your Context for Learning. Write continually throughout tasks 1–3 about each student. Determine how will you differentiate and support each identified student.

In summary, read, take notes, plan, write quality lesson plans, prepare, and film! You will be in a better position to address and write your edTPA responses.

Chapter 25

Get Your Feet Wet Early On

"To do anything truly worth doing, I must not stand back shivering and thinking of the cold and danger but jump in with gusto and scramble through as well as I can."—Og Mandino

As you begin student teaching, you may not feel ready to teach, but the best advice is to jump in headfirst and become an active member in the classroom from day one. This does not mean that you should teach a lesson on your first day; rather within your first few days, take steps toward a more active role in the classroom.

There are easy ways to take on an active role, short of teaching a lesson. For example, consider taking attendance for the classroom. Your cooperating teacher will undoubtedly be delighted if you take on this task because it can often feel like an unpleasant chore. You can turn this dull task into an opportunity to learn the students' names by making it into a game. While taking attendance, give yourself a point for each student's name you remember. Keep a tally as you work toward your goal of knowing 100 percent of the students' names.

Another way to create an active presence in the classroom is by moving around the classroom and initiating positive interactions with the students. The students are watching you, and when you are active—walking around the room, observing, assessing, and giving feedback—you show them that you are confident in yourself and your abilities. In essence, you are giving active signals to the students that you are ready for this role, and that you will be good at it. Conversely, if you are inactive, disappearing into the background, the students may see you as insecure and not up to the job, which will make it all that harder for you when you start teaching them.

Taking some responsibility for grading is another way to assert yourself in a positive way. Of course, you should ask for both permission and instructions from the cooperating teacher before you begin grading the students' work. To ensure fairness in assessment, the teacher probably uses a rubric, an answer sheet, or a baseline when grading, so you should use the same tools. Also, with grading comes the responsibility to give your students effective feedback. Strive to provide feedback that is clear, timely, and related to the students' growth, effort, and lesson objectives.

Finally, inquire with the cooperating teacher if there are opportunities to co-teach a part of a lesson. This co-teaching could include reviewing instructions, modeling some skill you want students to learn, doing a demonstration, or leading the assessment. This approach is an easy way to ease into teaching without feeling too much pressure initially.

Chapter 26

Learn Names Quickly

"Remember that a person's name is to that person the sweetest and most important sound in any language."—Dale Carnegie

There is a significant payoff in learning students' names and the correct pronunciation of the names as soon as you can. Learning names is a critical first step in building positive relationships with students. However, learning names and pronunciations can be challenging. In the first few weeks of the school year, teachers are typically bombarded with new names and faces: students, teachers, support staff, administration, parents, and the list goes on. At first, it is hard to retain all these new names, but with an applied effort over time, you will be able to remember the vast majority. There are steps you can take to help you in this effort.

MASTER PRONUNCIATIONS

To start, make every effort to pronounce the students' names correctly. Pronunciation matters greatly because this act shows respect and validates the students as individuals. Be preemptive by obtaining the student roster from your cooperating teacher and identifying any names you are unsure of how to pronounce. Ask the cooperating teacher for assistance in pronouncing names, or another helpful resource is the website *Pronounce Names* (https://www.pronouncenames.com), where you can type in students' names and hear the pronunciation (and variations).

As students share their names, be intentional in recording the names. One way is to spell the names phonetically. Repeat the name back to make sure you said it correctly. Alternatively, you may want to record students' names using a recorder on your phone. This could allow you to revisit students' names when you need a reminder. If you choose this option, be sure to ask permission from the cooperating teacher and the students and explain the reason why: You believe properly pronouncing their names is important.

EMBRACE THE SEATING CHART

A seating chart is an indispensable tool that will help you to remember your students' names. To save time, ask your cooperating teacher for a copy or spare seating chart. If the cooperating teacher does not have a seating chart, create your own. The simplest way to do this is by drawing one out on regular paper, writing in the students' names. If your cooperating teacher uses a learning management system, there may be a tool that allows you to create a seating chart. Other ideas to create seating charts abound on the Internet, especially on Pinterest.

In your first few weeks, keep the seating chart with you at all times (when grading, teaching, etc.). When calling on the students, use the seating chart to help remember students' names or to call on the students whom you frequently overlook. You should aim to call on every student, at a minimum, once every day.

PRACTICE SAYING NAMES EARLY AND OFTEN

Next, repetition is a great learning aid to learn students' names. Make a point of greeting your students by name when they enter the classroom or when you see them in the hallway. If you do not recall a student's name, politely ask them to remind you of his or her name. Or make a mental note of that student, and see where that student sits and refer to the seating chart. Follow up by calling on that student through the day to practice remembering the student's name.

Undoubtedly, you will sometimes call a student by the wrong name. Do not get discouraged; move past all your mistakes. In time, you will learn all their names. And you will quickly notice that the students will respond better when they know you know who they are and see them as valued members of the classroom. Simply put, it is important to the students, and they will appreciate your effort to get to know them. By doing so, you will develop a closer, more positive relationship with your students.

Finally, the effort to build rapport by learning names should extend outside your classroom. Begin by learning the names of your principal, assistant principals, team teachers, aides, parents, and volunteers. Eventually, widen your circle to include other teachers, custodians, and office support staff. Not only is this is a professional courtesy, but you are also more likely to receive needed help when you know the name of the person of whom you are asking a favor.

Chapter 27

Be Outstanding Inside and Outside of the Classroom

"There's a roughness and a surprising nature to most B movies that you don't get in classic films—something more immediate. I never chose those movies to leave impressions in my brain, they just did."—Tim Burton

Student teaching can lend itself as a golden opportunity in getting one step closer to landing your dream teaching job. Taking the "right step" and not a "misstep" boils down to making a unique and positive impression through your teaching and presence in the school community. If you are interested in working at the school where you are student teaching, keep in mind that principals often prefer to hire people they know and whose teaching abilities they trust. Therefore, going that extra step to ensure that the principal hears only positive feedback about you is critical. This is your time to stand out.

So, how does one stand out? Consider Tim Burton's quote about B movies at the beginning of this chapter. B movies, by definition, are not highly polished, but it is that unfinished quality and the surprises they often contain that leave an impression. You do not have to be the teacher candidate with the perfect grade point average to get stellar results and make a great impression. Instead, you have to put all your effort into producing and teaching an engaging, rigorous curriculum in an equitable, respectful classroom environment. Push yourself to be an innovator, a researcher of new ideas and best practices, and a calculated risktaker.

Consider the following questions to guide you as you design your lessons:

- How are you leveraging your knowledge of students' backgrounds, strengths, and interests to inform your lesson planning?
- Do the lessons have clear and understandable learning objectives?

- Are the learning objectives meaningful and connected to the students' lives?
- Are there a variety of methodologies to reach most of the diverse learners in the classroom?
- In what ways is the lesson going to be fun and engaging?
- Are you using alternative assessments (e.g., portfolios, performance assessments, conferences, etc.) to evaluate the students' learning?
- What is an idea that you can implement to make this an impressionable learning experience for the students?
- What are ways to extend this learning beyond the classroom to impact the broader community (e.g., service-learning project)?
- If you were a student, would this be a lesson you would like to experience?

Moving forward, know that planning, writing, and executing a thoughtful and innovative lesson is only one part of making a good impression during student teaching. As previously mentioned, principals are also looking for teachers who fit well with the culture of their school, as well as its students and staff. Student teaching is not just classroom teaching; it can serve as a testament to who you are as an educator, colleague, and advocate. Principals will be watching your involvement in the school and community just as much as your teaching. Here are ideas to make a great impression outside of the classroom:

- Attend all staff meetings and professional development with enthusiasm. Since you are the acting classroom teacher, you will be expected (if not required) to attend all of these meetings, so use them to your advantage. Network with other teachers. Try out strategies learned in the training while you are student teaching. Be an active participant in whole-group discussions about the school. Show the administrator(s) that you are fully invested in the school and its students, even if you are there only temporarily.
- Volunteer to take on additional responsibility. Perhaps your school has an upcoming concert, family night, fund-raiser, or other schoolwide event that you can help plan and execute. Teachers will appreciate the extra hand, and administrator(s) will appreciate your willingness to go the extra mile for their school, especially if it will directly benefit students and their families.
- Build a rapport with *all* staff and students. A warm, welcoming environment is a hallmark of a safe and thriving school community. Take time to learn the names of all staff (including support staff), and stop to say "Hello" when you see them around the school or take a moment to talk with them in staff common areas (lounge, office, etc.). Additionally, introduce yourself to other students you interact with around the school. Your students will most likely be talking about you to their friends, and all students are curious

about a new face in their school. As an educator, it is your responsibility to make every student feel welcome and safe at school.
- Reach out to other teachers or instructional coaches for insights. Your cooperating teacher is your mentor and your go-to, but don't discount the wealth of knowledge you will be surrounded with. Every teacher has their own unique style and perspective and is usually happy to share their insights and ideas with other educators (especially student teachers). Instructional coaches are another great source of information, as it is their sole job to help teachers teach. Principals appreciate when teachers are proactive and willing to reach out for help with something they are looking to improve upon. It shows the ability to be reflective, as well as to be open to feedback and to try something new for the benefit of their students.

As a final thought, while you want to impress through your teaching and school involvement, remember to remain true to yourself. Don't take on multiple extra projects or responsibilities if you will not be able to follow through. When you engage in conversations during meetings with other staff members, be genuine and honest; don't just say what you think people will want to hear. Strive to find the balance between moving out of your comfort zone and completely overextending yourself. These people may be your future colleagues and students, so be sure to showcase your professionalism right from the start.

Chapter 28

Use Classroom Management to Your Advantage

"It's hard to be fully creative without structure and constraint. Try to paint without a canvas. Creativity and freedom are two sides of the same coin. I like the best of both worlds. Want freedom? Get organized. Want to get organized? Get creative."—David Allen

Most student teachers enter their practicum concerned about classroom management. The anxiety they may feel stems from inexperience and a lack of understanding of how to effectively apply classroom management techniques to their teaching. Classroom management, as a whole, is a broad subject, and a thorough examination of all it encompasses is outside the scope of this book.

However, it is still important to understand the purpose and importance of its role in teaching. To begin, classroom management can be defined as a system of practices that increases learning, lowers behavioral problems, and, most importantly, communicates your expectations to your students. Successfully managing a classroom hinges on a combination of factors, including building positive relationships with students; maintaining set procedures and routines with consistency; and monitoring for engagement and compliance.

Keep in mind that as a student teacher, you will need to adhere to and respect the cooperating teacher's classroom management style. However, if you identify some classroom issues that interfere with the students' learning, then you can try various classroom management strategies to address the problem. In this section, you will find several quick and easy classroom management techniques that can be implemented at any grade level.

USE BELL WORK

One classroom management technique, applicable to K–12 grades, includes an exercise called "bell work," also known as entry tasks or morning work. Bell work is straightforward and can easily be modified based on what your class is currently learning. How it works is that, on a regular basis, students begin the class period or day by working on some sort of writing prompt, math problem, or other relevant tasks. Typically, this bell work is posted on the whiteboard or projected onto a screen using a computer or document camera. For example, upon their entering the class, you may have students respond to the following prompt: "We are learning about persuasion. Illustrate or write about a situation when you had to convince someone to do something."

This simple technique has many benefits: Bell work provides a consistent routine, so the students know what is expected of them from the minute they walk into the classroom; it reduces student misbehavior; and it shortens the time it takes to begin the class period or day. Bell work wakes up the brain and gets students in the mindset to learn. It can help spur students' interest in the day's lesson or encourage them to review information from previous lessons. Ideally, these tasks will also build on the students' background by connecting to their lives and their existing body of knowledge.

Giving students a set task at the beginning of the day gives you, the teacher, time to take care of administrative tasks such as taking attendance, lunch count, or even a moment to talk with a student one on one. Bell work also eliminates class downtime, which increases learning time for the students. Assume that a teacher working in a 180-day school uses bell work and reduces downtime by four minutes a day. This translates to an additional twelve hours of learning time for the students in a year. Using meaningful bell work in a consistent manner will lead to improved student learning and will reflect positively in your student teaching evaluations.

Be aware that bell work can quickly become stale or boring. To help keep the bell work fresh (and effective), invite students to assist you in developing future bell work tasks. Involving students in the creation process is just another way to give them more ownership over their learning, which can result in higher student engagement. Be sure to also provide student choice (e.g., ways of responding), as well as opportunities for social interaction. In short, strive to make bell work fun, authentic, and meaningful.

TRY A QUESTION AND CONCERN BOX

A question and concern box can also be an effective tool for classroom management. It gives students a way to express questions that may seem pressing to them but in a way that does not disrupt the flow of the lesson and class. The following example describes a student teacher's experience in implementing the question and concern box strategy.

> The student teacher was feeling frustrated when students would interrupt a class discussion or instructions with questions not relevant to the topic of discussion. The students' questions ranged from, "What is my grade in the class?" to "What homework do I need to make up?" While valid questions, they are not appropriate during classroom instruction or discussion time. Ultimately, the students' untimely questions reduced instruction time, detracted from meaningful class discussions, and negatively impacted the students' learning.
>
> To remedy this situation, the student teacher explained to the students that their questions and concerns were valid, but these types of questions would be handled with a question and concern box. Students were instructed to kindly write notes with their questions or concerns, place them in the box, and have a response from the student teacher within twenty-four hours. (For middle school students, writing a note was going to be no problem.)

At the primary level, students who struggle with reading or writing may be unable to write sentences to express their concerns or questions to you. However, with a few simple modifications, younger students can benefit from this technique as well. One idea is to give students access to different-colored sticky notes and explicitly teach students what each color means. For example, if students have a question they can use a yellow sticky note, for a concern or problem they need help with they use a blue sticky note, etc. The student can write their name and date on the note and stick it in a box or some other accessible place (like a laminated poster or a "jot lot" near your desk).

Another idea is to create a customized slip that students can fill out without having to write sentences. The slip would contain visuals that students can just circle or check off to express what they need. Again, you must explicitly teach students how and when to use the slips in order for the technique to work effectively. In addition, you must follow up with students in a timely and consistent manner; otherwise, this strategy will quickly lose its efficacy.

Overall, in using this strategy, you may find fewer students derailing group discussions with irrelevant questions and class instruction staying on point. Plus, students appreciate the personalized (and non-rushed) response, which can help to strengthen the teacher-student relationship.

MANAGING THE PAPERWORK

Student teachers often struggle to return graded papers. The amount of paperwork to be checked and properly graded can be overwhelming, even without trying to provide high-quality feedback on the students' work. Most student teachers do not have a plan for returning students' work in a timely fashion. Even work that is graded with feedback sits on the teacher's desk for too long. Feedback is more effective when delivered in a timely fashion, so creating a plan for grading and returning your students' work is crucial.

One approach to consider is inviting the few high-energy students (who may also be prone to misbehavior) to assist. Of course, you could have this role and responsibility rotate among all your students if you so choose. Let the students know you will put the graded feedback in a certain place or folder, ask the students to check this space or folder on a daily basis, and, if there's graded work, have the students automatically pass out the work at a specific time of the day.

To implement this approach, talk to students privately and express your need for their assistance. Typically, the students will be intrigued by the thought that a teacher needs help and will jump at this opportunity. If the students agree to help, the obvious benefit is that the students will burn off some energy, but more importantly, the student helpers will begin to view themselves as a valuable part of the classroom, which can help promote a more positive student identity. The increased involvement may also encourage the student helpers to participate more in other class activities. Finally, using this approach, the students' work with feedback will be returned in a timely and consistent manner.

MAXIMIZE CLASS TIME

Nothing will spin your classroom into chaos faster than completing a lesson plan five to ten minutes before the dismissal bell rings—thus creating downtime for the students. Devoting insufficient time for lesson planning can be a big mistake, and this lack of planning may quickly lead to student misbehavior. While you are distracted, mischievous children begin to move toward the door, others may begin to play-fight, and others will put their heads down. In any case, this downtime will result in a disengaged and chaotic classroom.

The good news is, with a little extra preparation and planning, you can transform class downtime into rich instructional and evaluative time. This can be accomplished by overplanning your lessons and having backup activities readily available. Consider planning for ten to fifteen minutes more instruction than you think you will need. Outlined below are several different ways to utilize this extra time:

- Plan a backup activity that can be easily modified based on your current lesson objectives. This can be a quick game, a think-pair-share, or some other activity that involves active responding from students.

- Use exit slips to have students reflect on and evaluate their learning. Review the lesson objectives, and ask students to complete a brief self-evaluation on whether they feel they have met the stated objectives, making sure to explain why or why not; or have them highlight an area of some learning or growth they achieved by noting some big takeaways. Alternatively, you can have students summarize their learning or pose clarifying questions that can be addressed the following day. As students leave the classroom, they hand you their feedback, allowing you to quickly assess their learning and make modifications for the following day's instruction.
- Outcome sentences are another useful strategy for evaluating learning and eliminating downtime at the end of a lesson. For this strategy, the teacher prepares various outcome sentences that can be posted on the wall or projected onto the board. The teacher then asks the students to write down and state an outcome sentence. This can be done individually, in partners/small groups, or as a whole class. Some examples would be: "I learned…," "I was surprised…," "I wonder…," "I think…" This quick and engaging activity allows students to think about their learning and share it with others. From the teacher's perspective, outcome sentences serve as an insightful evaluation tool to check students' understanding of the lesson.

BE CONSISTENT

Consistency is a common and critical thread woven into the fabric of effective classroom management. How you run your classroom communicates your expectations, and consistency is the driving force for accomplishing this. Students will be unable to identify their boundaries if you allow certain behaviors one day and then give consequences for the same behavior on a different day. Not only is it confusing for students, but they will quickly learn that when you ask them to do something, you don't really mean what you say. Consistency also communicates to students that the tasks you give them have purpose and meaning.

It is important to note that implementing and enforcing any kind of expectation can be messy, and consistency is the key to managing this. There may be chaos at first, but you still must give students a fair amount of time to process, learn, and practice these new expectations/approaches (i.e., new routine, procedure, process, or technique). You may feel a sense of frustration or helplessness if things are not going as you had planned (or hoped), but you must still continue using your chosen approach and monitoring the progress. If the results are unsatisfactory over time, then try adjusting your approach rather than abandoning it. Quickly abandoning the approach will again only communicate to students that you do not mean what you say and you will see behaviors and noncompliance begin to rise.

DEVELOP WITHITNESS

Build your capacity in becoming aware of what's happening in the classroom at all times, which is often referred to as having *withitness*. Student teachers may make the mistake of not taking the time to monitor for student compliance. It is all too tempting to give students a task and then immediately start bustling around the room. By doing this, you are inadvertently sending the message to students that getting to work right away is optional because you are not stopping long enough to make sure they do so.

To avoid falling prey to this temptation, employ a strategy called "Stand and Scan." This simple technique can be used at any time, at any grade level, and it is simple to implement. When giving directions, a task, or an assignment, send students off and then stand silently at the front of the classroom and watch. Do not allow students to come up to talk to you or ask questions, do not address the whole class, and do not move from your spot. Your job is to watch and wait for all students to follow your directions, which in turn communicates your expectations without having to say anything further.

Another integral part of this technique is to refrain from jumping on off-task behavior right away. Instead, watch the off-task student(s) for a minute or so, then approach them privately to remind them of your expectations. For example, imagine you hand out a math problem set and send students off to work, but one student is walking around talking to other students. She finally sits down, but then begins playing with objects in her desk. Calmly walk up to the student, physically point to the paper, and say, "The expectation is that you are working on your problem set," then walk away, return to the front of the room, and watch. Do not hover or nag; instead give the student a moment to process and start working. In addition, by returning to the front of the room, you are again communicating that the only option is compliance.

Be careful in implementing this technique, as it will require you to be aware of your implicit bias. All teachers carry with them implicit biases that influence teacher behaviors and actions, which, in turn, may adversely affect students, specifically students of color. It is imperative that you do this meaningful work around unpacking your implicit bias to ensure a healthy and equitable learning environment. A useful resource to learn more about checking your bias in the classroom is Teaching Tolerance (https://www.tolerance.org). Next, regularly reflect on how you are monitoring. For instance, ask yourself: "How am I ensuring that I am monitoring my students equitably? Or am I monitoring certain students (e.g., students of color in the class) more intensely and frequently than other students (e.g., white girls in the class)? Am I responding to all students who are in noncompliance in an equitable and dignified manner?"

It is important to note that while this strategy is simple in nature, it can sometimes be tricky to implement consistently. As a novice teacher, it may feel very uncomfortable to let the class feel chaotic while students settle. One way to combat this feeling is to time how long you are actually standing at the front of the room. It will *feel* like an eternity, but in reality, it is only a few minutes at the very most. Additionally, as with every other strategy outlined above, the more consistent you are about following through with this technique, the more clear your expectations will be to your students.

MASTER THE DAY-TO-DAY TASKS

As a closing thought, when preparing for student teaching, take time to think through how you will handle all the various day-to-day classroom tasks. For instance, when and how will you hand back papers? How will you take attendance? How will you manage makeup work? Be sure to utilize social media and other teacher-based resources such as Twitter, Pinterest, Teacher Channel website, etc. to give yourself some jumping-off points. Ultimately, your classroom management techniques should be tailored to you and your students. You will be unsuccessful if you choose strategies that you are unable to follow through with or implement correctly.

Effective classroom management also requires continuous problem-solving and experimentation, all while maintaining consistency and fairness. It requires you to be flexible and comfortable with trial and error. Lastly, keep in mind the importance and power of positive student-teacher relationships. Students' role in managing your classroom is critical; successful classroom management always starts with, and will be amplified by, the strong relationships you have built with your students.

Chapter 29

Know Yourself When It Comes to Discipline

"Know thyself."—Scribes of Dephi, via Plato

Classroom discipline is another robust topic that cannot be thoroughly examined in a book of this size. Nevertheless, the subject needs to be addressed because it is on the mind of practically every novice teacher. All educators know that at some point, no matter how great of a teacher you may be, discipline problems will arise.

Since all teachers inevitably face discipline challenges, how you handle them is critical to your professional growth. To establish a successful discipline policy, you will need a framework to work within. Construct this discipline framework by reflecting on your discipline philosophy and developing an understanding of the school rules, policies, and procedures.

REFLECT ON YOUR DISCIPLINE PHILOSOPHY

Begin by reviewing your education philosophy statement and asking yourself these questions:

- What values in your education philosophy translate into your beliefs about discipline?
- Does your discipline philosophy include such values as fairness, dignity, and equity?
- Using five adjectives, how would you describe your classroom discipline philosophy?

Jot down your ideas and begin drafting your discipline philosophy. Your discipline philosophy will allow you to build on your strengths and beliefs to maintain order in your classroom while ensuring the dignity of your students. While you are doing this exercise, also ask yourself if you are going to be democratic, authoritarian, or moderate in your discipline approach. For example, if you are by nature laid-back and you desire a democratic approach to classroom management and discipline, then taking on the role as an authoritarian will be exhausting and self-defeating. Since you will probably not be able to maintain that authoritarian mask, the students may hear the authoritarian verbal tone but receive a very different (mixed) message from your nonverbal cues. The possible anxiety and confusion caused by mixed signals may lead to classroom management issues. In short, mixed signals, and the classroom misbehavior that may result, can be avoided by establishing a classroom discipline philosophy and approach that is consistent with who you are. And this is accomplished through ongoing self-reflection.

KNOW THE SCHOOL RULES, POLICIES, AND PROCEDURES

A second and relatively easy step to take to ease your discipline anxiety is to know the rules, policies, and procedures of the school. Begin your research by reviewing the school's handbook to become familiar with its stated policies. Many schools have electronic versions of their handbooks posted on their websites. If you cannot locate one online, then ask your cooperating teacher or school administration for a copy. The handbook is a valuable resource for information on schedules, mission and belief statements, staff contacts, technology, and emergency guidelines, as well as discipline. It should provide a sufficient explanation of school policies on the following:

- Classroom infractions
- Dress code
- Drugs and alcohol
- Due process
- Insubordination
- Physical and verbal abuse
- Tardiness and absences
- Weapons

Being intentional about how your discipline philosophy and having a richer understanding of the rules and policies in the school are valuable starting points to grow your ability to have an orderly and dignified classroom environment. Lastly, know that, as with every other aspect in teaching, your discipline philosophy and approach may change over time based on new experiences. Based on your learnings and growth as an educator and the group of students in front of you, you may need (or want) to refine your discipline philosophy and approach.

SUGGESTED READING

Richard L. Curwin, Allen N. Mendler, and Brian D. Mendler, *Discipline with Dignity, 4th Edition: How to Build Responsibility, Relationships, and Respect in Your Classroom* (Alexandria: ASCD, 2018).

Chapter 30

Think Customer Service

"A satisfied customer is the best business strategy of all."—Michael Leboeu

Another great way to differentiate yourself from other student teachers is to view your practicum through a customer service lens. The teaching profession requires the utmost professionalism when dealing with your colleagues, your students, and their families. In many ways, dealing with them is no different from dealing with customers you would encounter in any other profession. Below are five traits that define excellent customer service and ways that you can incorporate them into your teaching practices:

- Competence
- Responsiveness
- Friendliness
- Listening
- Proactiveness

COMPETENCE

As a student teacher, even though you are still learning the ropes, it is important to make every attempt to come across as the competent and professional educator that you are in every interaction with a parent or guardian. If the parent or guardian challenges you on a certain decision, remain calm and professional by supporting your decision with research or evidence. Oftentimes there may be a disagreement if parents are feeling that they are not being heard, so sometimes the best option is just to listen. Parents want to know you are truly listening to their concerns and that you are trying to understand where they are coming from. When you slow down to hear their side of the situation and can reasonably support your decision, the parent or guardian will likely side with you or respectfully disagree.

RESPONSIVENESS

Next, when responding to inquiries from the students' families, timing is key. Regular and open communication with parents or guardians is an essential part of the job, so getting into the habit of responding as soon as you can to their questions or concerns is crucial. Make a concerted effort to check your voice mail daily and your emails several times a day. Getting into this habit early and often will serve you well in student teaching and throughout your teaching career as well. If you need to do further research to answer a question, simply call or email the parent or guardian and let them know that you received their message, that you are looking into their issue, and that you will get back to them shortly.

If you do not respond within a reasonable time, you risk the guardian taking his or her inquiry to another teacher or the school administration, which can reflect poorly on you. More importantly, understand that families talk to each other, and if they feel they were ignored, they will quickly let others know about it. This could negatively impact your relationships with other student families as well.

FRIENDLINESS

It is important to convey a sense of friendliness in every interaction with parents and guardians, even on your toughest days. Every single person has things going on in their lives; it is never okay to impose your bad mood on others. A simple smile or a wave hello is really all it takes to show friendliness to others. Of course, always remain true to yourself, and be careful not to be overly friendly either, as this can come across as insincere. With regard to phone conversations, an easy technique to convey friendliness is to smile while you are talking. Your smile will come through in your voice and inflections.

LISTENING

As educators, the ability to truly listen to others is one of our most valuable and necessary tools. Many of the situations you will encounter in your teaching career will call for you to be able to pause and listen without judgment, whether it's to a parent concerned about a child's academic performance, or a grandmother concerned about a grandchild's possible gang involvement, or a student emotionally distraught because of peer bullying. Oftentimes, just the act of listening without offering up advice or solutions is exactly what the other party needs to release some of their pent-up frustrations or fears. Once those feelings have been aired, a true conversation can begin between you and all parties concerned.

PROACTIVENESS

The final trait that characterizes fabulous customer service is being proactive—anticipating your customers' needs and responding to them. Being proactive is an important part of teaching, especially when dealing with students' families. For instance, one of the top needs of parents and guardians is being informed of their child's social well-being and academic performance.

A first step to being proactive is to ask the communication preferences of the parents and guardians: in person, phone calls, emails, other written forms (e.g., newsletters, letters, notes), text messages, social media (e.g., a professional-only Twitter account), or specific teacher and parent communication apps (e.g., the Remind app). Next, taking into account the families' preferences and the pressing demands on your time, establish a communication schedule that is reasonable. Frequent (however you define this) and consistent communication is key.

Another approach is to communicate early and often when a student begins to show signs of poor performance or when other concerns surface. Even if it feels like a small problem, do not hesitate to reach out. This communication will often open up a dialogue between you and the family. Conveying your care and concern, even over the small things, shows guardians that you are fully invested in their child's success. Parents will appreciate your honesty and can be your biggest ally when deciding on appropriate interventions for their child. Also, having proactive communication protects you by having your observations and concerns on record.

Overall, taking a proactive approach as a teacher candidate will differentiate you from your peers and will provide you with concrete evidence of your communication skills with parents and guardians that may help in a later interview.

Chapter 31

Build Your Touchstone

"Desire is the key to motivation, but it's determination and commitment to an unrelenting pursuit of your goal—a commitment to excellence—that will enable you to attain the success you seek."—Mario Andretti

As previously discussed throughout this section, your student teaching experience will present you with numerous opportunities to differentiate yourself from fellow teacher candidates. Another great way to further set yourself apart is by establishing a touchstone as you enter student teaching. A touchstone is a standard by which something is judged. Therefore, the touchstone you establish should be a standard of excellence that is used to improve targeted student learning, through instruction or a curriculum, and that is easily transferable to another school.

In today's schools, you will find there is a strong emphasis on student achievement, and therefore school administrators are seeking out job candidates who can effectively plan, instruct, and assess, as well as be reflective of their pedagogy. Administrators are looking for specific examples of how you have improved student learning and ways you could incorporate those same practices to make a positive impact on student learning in their schools. As you embark on student teaching, consider these tips in creating your touchstone.

IDENTIFY AREAS OF IMPROVEMENT

In establishing your touchstone, you should begin by focusing most of your effort in improving one particular area. Use student data, such as student work or schoolwide standardized testing, to determine your focus area.

For example, let us imagine that you have scrutinized your school's recent standardized test scores. You notice that in the areas of writing and math, the students' scores have progressed significantly from last year. However, the reading scores showed only slight improvement and continue to lag behind the district and state average scores. From this data, you resolve to incorporate reading skills in your curriculum in hopes of increasing students' reading comprehension, and, ultimately, the students' test results.

ESTABLISH A BASELINE

The next step is to establish a starting point (a baseline) for your area of improvement. This step of having a baseline assessment will 1) determine the skill level in your particular classroom and 2) create a standard through which you can measure progress. In short, understanding your baseline will allow you to measure your students' growth. Here are some assessment approaches to determine a baseline of the students' learning and skill level:

- Teacher-student interview/conferences
- Classroom-based assessments (e.g., quizzes and tests)
- Sample student work
- Surveys
- Standardized tests
- Student reflections
- Teacher observations

Illustrative Example

Imagine you quiz your students on an article they just read. After the quiz, you survey the students by asking them to identify the different reading strategies they employed while reading the article. Your survey lists various best-practice reading strategies with descriptive examples, and the students mark the ones they used. From the collected surveys, you build your baseline by formulating some quantitative findings. For instance, you determine that only 15 percent of your students use two or more of the best-practice reading strategies. In addition, 65 percent of the students indicated they had "difficulty" in comprehending the article.

Next, you grade the quizzes and find a class average score of 62 percent. The survey findings shed some light as to why the students scored poorly on the reading comprehension quiz. You realize that the students use very few reading strategies to improve their comprehension, and this is reflected in their assessments. The good news is that you have a clearer view of the problem and you have a measurable baseline (the quantitative analysis) to determine if using reading strategies will improve the students' reading comprehension.

BUILD YOUR TOUCHSTONE

As a first step in building your touchstone, you must become a reflective problem-solver. Begin by brainstorming different ways to tackle the problem of improving your students' baseline. Consider incorporating best practices learned in your teacher education training. Another great way to figure out how to implement effective strategies is in collaborating with other teachers. For instance, if improving reading comprehension was my focus, then I would partner with the language arts teachers or reading specialists to investigate effective reading strategies. There are other means to generate your plan of action:

- Reading literature
- Researching educational journals
- Observing classrooms in which students are exhibiting proficiency in your area of improvement
- Partnering with your local university
- Attending professional development workshops
- Searching the Internet

Once you have determined the best practice instructional strategies and/or changes to make in your curriculum, the next step is implementation. For instance, referencing back to the earlier reading comprehension example, you may begin to teach the students how to monitor their reading comprehension, employ "fix- it" strategies when the students' comprehension falls off, and introduce additional tools discovered during your research.

Soon after implementation, monitor and evaluate your plan of action to see if what you are doing is influencing the bottom line: your students' learning. Using the same assessment tools (in this example, a survey and a quiz), you develop a quantitative analysis. Compared to the baseline, have the students shown any significant improvement in your targeted area of improvement, such as reading comprehension?

Lastly, as you gather formative evidence, be reflective and regularly modify your plan of action to get even greater results. Consider additional support and feedback you could provide students who are not experiencing the expected level of growth in their learning.

COMMUNICATING YOUR TOUCHSTONE

If you are able to accomplish this feat during your already hectic student teaching time, then consider yourself a teaching rock star. And you have a concrete example of student improvement to discuss at future job interviews. In such discussions, articulate the steps you took: collecting and analyzing the data, setting student-focused learning goals, researching the methodology, implementing your plan, and evaluating and reflecting on the results. Describe how this process impacted student learning by providing a mix of qualitative and quantitative findings.

Finally, show how the expectations you set at the school where you were as a student teacher could be applicable to other schools. For instance, "Reviewing the state tests, I [the job candidate] noticed the students' reading scores at your [the principal's] school are similar to the school where I was a student teacher. I strongly believe I would be able to deliver the same improvements in reading comprehension to ABC School as I did in XYZ School." In summary, having a touchstone of excellence will greatly enhance your chances of being hired in the school you desire.

Chapter 32

How to Approach the edTPA Writing

"You don't start out writing good stuff. You start out writing crap and thinking it's good stuff, and then gradually you get better at it. That's why I say one of the most valuable traits is persistence."—Octavia E. Butler

Writing for the edTPA is a challenging and time-consuming endeavor that will require patience and tenacity to complete. As a first step, begin by writing out thorough and high-quality lesson plans for the learning segment. Try to be as detailed as possible by including potential dialogue and being sure to outline and highlight any planned supports or assessments you will be using. Once you have written your lesson plans and taught and filmed the lesson segment, it is time to start unpacking and analyzing your teaching.

Next, due to the sheer amount of writing you will be doing, it is imperative to schedule your edTPA writing into reasonable chunks. It is unwise to attempt any sort of marathon writing right before your submission deadline. Doing so will leave you frustrated and unable to complete the writing in a manner that is satisfactory. Depending on your schedule, attempt to write for a few hours a day, being sure to take frequent mental and physical breaks. This writing routine may last several weeks, and while it may be tempting to push through and finish as quickly as possible, remember the boundaries you have set for yourself. Working on such an extensive project without giving your mind and body ample time to rest will only be a disservice to you and your writing. It is also useful to reflect on what types of places will help you be the most productive in your writing. Whether you choose your kitchen table or a coffee shop, make an effort to work on your writing in a space that is calm and relatively free from distractions.

To guide your writing, regularly use the edTPA's *Understanding Rubric Level Progressions* handbook for your focus area. This edTPA resource is extremely helpful and should not be overlooked. To use it effectively, start by reading through the *Understanding Rubric Level Progressions* handbook to gain a better understanding of what each rubric entails. With those guidelines in mind, write your initial responses to the edTPA writing prompts. Then, reread what the edTPA scores will be looking for at level 3 and 4 for each rubric and reflect on the quality of your response compared to the rubric expectations. When reflecting and comparing, here are additional thoughts to consider:

- Does the writing fully answer each prompt? Many of the prompts will have more than one part that must be addressed in your response. For example, the question may ask you to describe and justify supports for "the whole class, individuals, and/or groups of students with specific learning needs." It will therefore be expected of you to outline this information for each one of these groups to sufficiently answer the prompt.
- Be aware of your audience and strive for clarity. Avoid using educational jargon and acronyms such as SEL, EL, etc. Instead, write out *social emotional learning* or *English learner* and be sure to provide as much as context as possible.
- If the prompt includes a bulleted list, be sure to address each bullet point fully in a separate paragraph within the prompt. Remember, the goal is to keep your writing clear and concise.
- Don't forget to justify and back up your instructional moves with educational learning theories where applicable. If you come to a prompt that specifically asks you to use principles from research and/or theory to support your justifications, you must do so or risk receiving a failing score. Outlined below is a list of educational learning theories to research and potentially use in your edTPA™ writing:
  - Active engagement
  - Behaviorism
  - Comprehension instruction
  - Constructivism
  - Memory
  - Schema theory
  - Spiral curriculum
  - The role of language
  - Zone of proximal development

In general, the writing process takes time, it is challenging, and you have to be accepting of this reality before you begin. Remember that while you will want to regularly push yourself, you must continue to take care of you. One teacher candidate nicely summed up the writing process in this way:

> You are going to want to cry, pull your hair out, doubt you should even be a teacher, convince yourself you're going to fail, but that's all part of the journey. If you need to take a break from writing, take a break. Remember self-care. If you hit a wall, it's okay to stop. I hit many walls along the way and that's normal.

In summary, one must first acknowledge and accept the demanding nature of this endeavor by setting boundaries before diving in. Once you are ready to begin, start with high-quality and detailed lesson plans, establish a consistent writing routine early on, and leverage the edTPA's *Understanding Rubric Level Progressions* handbook throughout the entire writing process. These simple yet practical strategies will put you in a more solid position to successfully address the writing component of your edTPA portfolio.

Chapter 33

Thank Your Network

"Gratitude is the fairest blossom which springs from the soul."—Henry Ward Beecher

In the flurry of wrapping up your final days of student teaching, be sure to take some time to begin thanking all of the individuals who provided you with support along the way. Review your network list and take note of all those you wish to thank, being sure to jot down specifically what they did for you or in what ways they supported you. Doing this will help organize your thoughts around whom you need to thank and how you would like to do so.

Gratitude comes in many forms. A thank-you can be in the form of a card, a simple note, or a gift—but ultimately what truly matters is that it is a meaningful, heartfelt gesture. We all have people around us who go the extra mile without being asked, and how you thank each person should reflect that.

In practicing gratitude, try starting with deciding on how to thank your cooperating teacher. Take into consideration the countless hours he or she spent mentoring you in lesson planning, grading papers, making copies, or dealing with parents and difficult students, not to mention all of the other little, yet essential, things they taught you along the way. Then from there, begin thinking outward. Perhaps the teacher next door was an invaluable partner to you or the school secretary had your back every time you needed help with administrative tasks.

For your cooperating teacher, members of your grade-level team, field supervisor, and other staff members who helped you, a small, thoughtful gift with a handwritten card would be a kind gesture. When filling out the card, take time to think about your interactions with these individuals and let them know just how much they have affected you or helped shape your teaching practices. Now is not the time for generic cookie-cutter thank-you notes; be specific and genuine. When buying gifts, be mindful of the person for whom you are buying. For example, don't buy Starbucks gift cards for people who don't drink coffee. When in doubt, a bouquet of flowers or a potted plant is a universal gift that can easily be customized and is always well-received.

Don't forget to show your gratitude to your students and their families. Remember that even though you were there only for a short time, your presence will have deeply affected your students. They will feel a strong bond with you and will miss having you there every day. They, just like adults, will need closure and time to properly say good-bye. Your thank-you to them does not need to be fancy or complicated, but it should be thoughtful. For example, one of my colleagues wrote an individualized thank-you note to each of her students as her sendoff. Another option is to send out a mass communication (via a personalized letter sent home or by email) to the students and their families, thanking them for their partnership and expressing your gratitude for the important role they played in your student teaching experience.

Finally, keep in mind those closest to you, such as your family and friends. They are the ones who will most likely have taken the brunt of all your rants and stress over the past several months. They are often the bedrock of our lives and need to be reminded of how important they are to us. The greatest gift you can give those who are your biggest supporters is your time. When your practicum ends, be sure to slow down and make an effort to spend quality time with your family and friends as a way to say thank you, which also is a much-needed act of self-care.

Section III

FIND YOUR IDEAL TEACHER JOB

Chapter 34

Continue to Shine After Student Teaching

"It takes a long time to educate a community, and it can't be done by spellbinders, moneybags, hypnotizers, magicians, or Aladdin's lamp. Character is what matters on a paper."—Harry J. Grant

Well done—you have completed your student teaching experience! As student teaching winds down and you prepare for graduation, you may experience some relative calm before the hiring season picks up. School districts will be on the lookout for potential employees starting as early as March, going all the way through to August. During this period, you can increase your chances of being hired by actively networking and diversifying your skill sets.

SEEK PROFESSIONAL DEVELOPMENT

In the first section of the book *Leverage Your Teacher Education Training*, teacher candidates were encouraged to improve in their growth areas, specifically pertaining to content knowledge and pedagogy. Now, as you have completed your practicum, reflect on your student teaching experience, and ask what areas in your practice could be strengthened through targeted professional development. Classes and micro-credentials may serve as professional development opportunities.

Enrolling in additional classes through your higher education institute or another education organization may broaden your skills and knowledge. Consider pursuing additional endorsements or certification in high-need areas such as ELL (English language learners) or special education. Even if you do not earn an endorsement or certification, there are numerous benefits to taking additional courses. For one, you will know more about how to meet your students' learning needs. Next, you will also have a strong foundation should you decide, in the future, to pursue extra certification. Extra courses will also make you more appealing to principals and hiring committees.

Micro-credentials are another venue for you to learn a specific skill or knowledge, demonstrate competency related to this skill or knowledge, and earn a digitized form of certification. There are many organizations and platforms that offer education-related micro-credentials at a reasonable cost, such as the National Education Association and Digital Promise. When you choose a micro-credential you want to pursue based on your teaching and student needs, often there are curated resources and readings to guide your learning. In many cases, once you earn your micro-credential, you will receive a digital badge that you can include on your resume or LinkedIn profile—again further differentiating yourself from other teacher candidates.

SUBSTITUTE-TEACH OR COACH

You may be thinking "No more coursework!" and this is completely understandable. The good news is that there are many other ways to increase your value as a job candidate that do not require you to take classes or write papers. Substitute teaching and coaching are excellent ways to strengthen your teaching skills and get the proverbial "foot in the door." They both provide real-world experiences working with students that will extend your skills beyond your practicum experience. While substitute-teaching and coaching, this is an excellent time to continue expanding your network.

Remember to keep records on the teachers and schools you substituted in, and organizational tools such as your network spreadsheet will make this a breeze (see the *Organize Your Contacts* strategy, in section I). Also, while teaching or coaching, remember to try to become a familiar face in the school (see the *Benefit from Networking in Schools* strategy, in section I).

VOLUNTEER

If you cannot find a substitute teaching or coaching position, then consider becoming active in your local community. Teachers are known for their commitment to their communities. Many teachers and administrators volunteer great amounts of their time for causes that are important to them. Find a cause that you are passionate about, such as homelessness, hunger, the environment, or local school improvement. Start by calling your local city government, or visiting their website, to get a list of volunteer opportunities that might interest you, such as the Boy/Girl Scouts, Rotary Clubs, Kiwanis, YMCA, Red Cross, and United Way. You may find yourself rubbing shoulders with people in positions who can help you obtain that desired teacher job. In addition to helping the community, you are building and using your skills, networking with others, and polishing your résumé to reflect your civic-minded activities.

Chapter 35

Craft an Effective Résumé

"The résumé explains your experience, what kinds of classes you taught, your school improvement, and any cocurricular activities you directed. The résumé will help make the final sale to secure a place on the interview list."—Robert W. Pollock, Ed.D.

As you begin crafting your résumé, you may be wondering where to start and what to include. There is a vast amount of resources out there on résumé writing, including hundreds of books and magazine articles, countless websites, and numerous career workshops devoted to this topic alone. However, the aim here is to provide you with a simple approach to building your résumé, as well as some helpful and constructive tips to help make it a shining reflection of your abilities and experience.

When thinking about what to include on your résumé, remember that it serves two important functions. First, it highlights your achievements (both professional and academic) as well as your involvement in the community. Second, your résumé shows to prospective employers all the ways in which you are qualified to fulfill the position(s) you are seeking. A well-crafted résumé should highlight the precise skills and expertise you possess that would meet the specifications for the job you desire. Hence, it should come as no surprise that because of your diverse background of experiences, you will need more than one version of your résumé. Each position of interest will present its own unique set of duties and responsibilities, and you will want a résumé that speaks to the requirements of each particular position.

Every résumé has the same components—contact information, education, and experience. Your résumé may also have:

- Personal contact information
- Objective

- Education and certification
- Work experience

PERSONAL CONTACT INFORMATION

This section is self-explanatory; it should include your name, address, phone number, email address (make sure it is professional-sounding), your public LinkedIn profile link, and any information that you think would assist an administrator or hiring committee in contacting you. Please note that if you are working from an older résumé template, you should check that your information is correct.

TEXTBOX 35.1   EXAMPLE OF THE CONTACT INFO SECTION OF A RÉSUMÉ

TAYLOR C. DOE
1234 8th Avenue   Tel: (312) 555-1234
Chicago, IL 60120   johna1234@gmail.com
LinkedIn: www.linkedin.com/in/taylordoe1

OBJECTIVE

It is not essential to include a career objective in your résumé. More and more experts are saying that an objective is a waste of scarce space that could be used to highlight another skill or accomplishment. On the other hand, some hiring managers prefer résumés with an objective because it allows them to easily sort and file résumés according to job openings. If you include one, your objective statement should be concise and specific to the job for which you are applying. The example objective statement in Textbox 35.2 is right to the point and lets the hiring manager know what the job seeker wants.

TEXTBOX 35.2   EXAMPLE OF AN OBJECTIVE ON A RÉSUMÉ

Objective

Culturally responsive educator seeking a social studies teacher position in the Chicago Public Schools

EDUCATION AND CERTIFICATION

Include here the degrees you have received, name(s) of the school(s) you graduated from, dates of graduation, and any other studies that contribute to your qualifications as a teacher. If you do not have a lot of work experience, then highlight your academic successes, such as awards or honors you have received. Include your GPA only if it is 3.0 or higher. Textbox 35.3 illustrates one way to format the education and certification section of a résumé.

TEXTBOX 35.3   EXAMPLE OF THE EDUCATION AND CERTIFICATION SECTION OF A RÉSUMÉ

Education and Certification

Master of Arts in Teaching   Chicago, IL
Loyola University   May 2020

Bachelor of Arts in Education   Chicago, IL
DePaul University   May 2017

Illinois Teaching Certificate
Effective 2017–2027 Endorsements in Social Studies and ELL

EXPERIENCE

In many résumés, this section is often too cumbersome and wordy. Some misguided job seekers believe their chances are diminished if they have not listed all their skills and experiences. On the contrary, the purpose of your résumé is to highlight your most important skills and experiences and show how they relate to the job for which you are applying. You can discuss your skills and experience in more depth during your interview.

Additionally, hiring administrators have limited time, and they may skip over long-winded explanations of work history. In writing your résumé, prioritize your most important skills and experiences, highlighting them with bullets. Try to emphasize accomplishments and achievements. Numbers and percentages tend to jump out to résumé reviewers. Be concise and clear in your writing, using action words to begin each skill and experience. Textbox 35.4 provides a bulleted example of a teacher experience section of a résumé. Table 35.1 shows teacher-specific action verbs to assist in your résumé writing.

Table 35.1 Action Verbs for a Teacher Résumé

Abstracted	Conceived	Instituted	Provided
Achieved	Conducted	Integrated	Publicized
Acquired	Conserved	Investigated	Published
Acted	Consulted	Judged	Received
Adapted	Contracted	Kept	Reduced
Addressed	Contributed	Launched	Referred
Administered	Counseled	Learned	Related
Advertised	Created	Mentored	Relied
Advised	Critiqued	Met	Reported
Advocated	Cultivated	Minimized	Researched
Applied	Dealt	Modeled	Responded
Appraised	Designed	Modified	Restored
Approved	Detected	Monitored	Revamped
Arranged	Determined	Narrated	Set goals
Ascertained	Developed	Negotiated	Shaped
Augmented	Devised	Observed	Skilled
Authored	Established	Obtained	Strategized
Bolstered	Estimated	Offered	Solved
Briefed	Evaluated	Operated	Strengthened
Brought	Examined	Ordered	Stressed
Budgeted	Exceeded	Organized	Studied
Built	Excelled	Originated	Substantiated
Calculated	Expanded	Practiced	Succeeded
Cared	Expedited	Predicted	Summarized
Chaired	Experimented	Prepared	Synthesized
Collaborated	Explained	Presented	Supervised
Collected	Explored	Prioritized	Supported
Comforted	Expressed	Produced	Surveyed
Communicated	Extracted	Programmed	Sustained
Compared	Facilitated	Projected	Symbolized
Completed	Fashioned	Promoted	Tabulated
Complied	Influenced	Proposed	Talked
Composed	Initiated	Protected	Taught
Computed	Inspected	Proved	Visualized

TEXTBOX 35.4   EXAMPLE OF TEACHING EXPERIENCE ON A RÉSUMÉ

Teaching Experience

ABC High School, Seattle, WA
Business Education Teacher September 2006–Present

- Teaches Introduction to Information Technology and Business Law
- Advises school's business club, Future Business Leaders of America and grew the club 145%

- Using new reading strategies, improved reading scores by 23% on standardized tests
- Won Seattle Rotary's Teacher of the Month (October 2017)

ADDITIONAL RÉSUMÉ ADVICE

Ultimately, your résumé should be a one-page reflection of you and everything you can offer to a prospective employer. All of the work that goes into preparing a résumé is crucial, from what information to include (or leave out), down to the style and layout. Consider getting outside opinions on how to improve your résumé by asking your program's career counselor, trusted education professionals, colleagues, family, and friends. Finally, before you send your résumé to prospective employers, proofreading it multiple times. Each time you read through, carefully check for spelling and grammatical errors, as many employers will just toss out any résumé with such errors.

Chapter 36

A Career Counselor's Perspective

Career Advice

Angela Engel, Career Counselor

Meet with your college career counselor before applying for teaching positions or attending a career fair. In addition to reviewing your résumé, career counselors may provide insider information on the districts to which you are applying, such as what to highlight in your customized cover letter; and they can connect you with the recruiters from your top districts.

I recommend teacher candidates apply for positions using the online application tracking system *and* send their electronic résumé individually, along with a personalized note letting them know you have applied, to the following people: 1) the recruiter; 2) the administrator; 3) the department chair or lead teacher; and if possible, 4) the school's office manager/administrator's administrative assistant.

Sending emails to everyone involved in the hiring process lets them know you are deeply interested in their school, and it prevents your résumé from potentially getting lost in the applicant-tracking system. How will you know your résumé is working? You will know your résumé is working if it starts generating interviews. The purpose of the résumé is to open the door to interviews.

Don't wait to start preparing for interviews! You should begin preparing for interviews *before* you start applying for jobs. The phone could ring within minutes of your submitting your résumé (not always, but it does happen!). Keep reading this book on how to prepare for your teaching interviews, and participate in a practice interview with your career counselor.

Chapter 37

Ask (the Right Person) for Help on Your Résumé

"Anything that's worth having is worth asking for. Some say yes and some say no."—Melba Colgrove

A bold but creative strategy is to meet with an administrator to review your résumé and cover letter—ideally at the school where you student taught. An administrator's time is very valuable, so when requesting a meeting, be sure to contact the administrator's secretary to set this up for you. Once the meeting is scheduled, reach out to the administrator via email to let them know the reason for the meeting and some of the things you would like to discuss with them.

In preparation for your meeting, make sure to bring with you a hard copy of your résumé and cover letter (or send one electronically ahead of the meeting to the administrator). Doing so will not only showcase your professionalism, it shows the administrator you value their time and expertise by being prepared. Also, come to the meeting with specific questions in hand to make the most of your time. In the end, thank the administrator for meeting with you and let them know that you appreciate his or her valuable insight on how to improve the effectiveness of your résumé and cover letter.

There are some real benefits to having face time with a school administrator. The first and most obvious benefit of arranging this meeting is to receive feedback from the type of person who will be hiring you. Try to bring an extra draft of your documents for you to make notes on as you review them. In the course of your conversation, solicit specific suggestions to improve your résumé and cover letter.

A less obvious benefit of this strategy is that when meeting with the administrator, the conversation centers on you and your qualifications. As a result, this conversation might just be the catalyst that shifts the administrator's thinking of you as a "teacher candidate" to a "highly qualified job candidate." If this shift occurs, the administrator may divulge job leads to you, or might even go as far as putting in a good word for you at another hiring school.

Lastly, to take full advantage of your time with the administrator, spend a few moments gathering their insights on the interview process. A shining résumé and cover letter won't get you very far without a stellar interview to back it up. Therefore, this is a golden opportunity for you to get yourself one step ahead of other potential job candidates. For example, you may be curious about what interview questions are commonly asked for the position you are seeking. More often than not, administrators will share with you a few of the top interview questions, or at a minimum, provide you clues as to what topics are typically discussed and how to approach them. This is also a great time to inquire about what qualities they are looking for when interviewing job applicants.

If for some reason you are not able to arrange a meeting with the administrator, then attempt to connect with others in your school network: teacher colleagues, librarians, cooperating teacher, professors, and clinical supervisors. They may have served on hiring committees and be able to provide you with unique perspectives.

Chapter 38

Learn from Your Work Experience

"In wisdom gathered over time I have found that every experience is a form of exploration."—Ansel Adams

As you refine your résumé and seek advice on how to improve it, also take time to reflect on all your work experiences, regardless of whether these experiences are directly related to education or not. Work experience looks fantastic on a résumé and helps you answer such interview questions as:

- What were some important lessons you learned from your experiences?
- What are the skills you possess that will assist you as a teacher? Why?
- What is a challenge you faced, and how you did you overcome it?
- How are you different from the other job candidates?

Your work experiences provide an additional and unique window for interviewers to evaluate you. Use this to your advantage. Differentiate yourself from other candidates by talking about your work experiences and demonstrating how those experiences make you a stronger teacher. If your work experiences were in the field of education, reflect on these real-life experiences and the unique insights you learned that could be applied to your future teaching career.

If you have work experiences that are not directly related to education, for example, you were a barista or a retail store manager, attempt to connect your experience to teaching. For instance, in your job, were you a team player or leader? These questions are asking about your disposition and skill sets, and they are important because, as an educator, you will be collaborating with colleagues, or you may have to lead a new initiative at the school. Or, if your work experiences involved customer service, think about what lessons from providing customer service could be applied to serving your students and their families. In short, upon reflecting on your work experiences, be prepared to explain to the interviewer how you will utilize those experiences and skills to maximize student learning and growth.

Extracting meaning from your work experience and reflecting on how it applies to your teaching is a meaningful activity in preparing for an interview. Think back on your experiences, review the interview questions below (perhaps using these as prompts for your journal), and determine how your experiences will better position you as a job candidate.

- What were some important lessons you learned from your past work experiences?
- What are the skills you possess that will assist you in teaching?
- What is a challenge you faced, and how did you overcome it?
- How are you different from the other job candidates?

Chapter 39

Be Aware of the Hiring Time Frame

"A goal without a plan is just a wish."—Antoine de Saint-Exupéry

Inevitably, a pressing question on most every future teacher's mind will be, "When should I begin looking for a teaching job?" To help you plan for this venture, outlined below is a breakdown of the typical hiring conditions, beginning in March and leading up to the start of the next academic year. Along with the hiring timetable, you will find concrete actions that any soon-to-be teacher can take to improve the likelihood of being hired.

MARCH AND APRIL

March and April are great months to start browsing job listings to find out what positions are available. Carefully check to see if the open positions are for the current year or the next school year. While browsing the job openings, keep track of which positions are in higher demand and in what schools. (See the strategy *Track Your Job Search* later in this section.) Carefully read the descriptions that accompany each job opening to find out any specific certification requirements and to get a feel for what employers are looking for in an ideal job candidate. While taking this proactive step, be aware that some school districts will not consider applications for the next school year until after a certain date, and April may be too early.

MAY AND JUNE

May and June are typically the busiest months for hiring teachers. Many district recruiters and school administrators consider this time frame to be their biggest and best opportunity for attracting and hiring quality teachers from the available teacher-candidate pool. Many administrators express that if they wait until July or August to begin hiring, the applicant pool will be much smaller, and it will be more difficult to find highly qualified teachers. In addition, as the school year ends, teachers officially announce retirements, transfers, or resignations, so administrators want to move quickly to fill these vacancies.

JULY

Hiring activity will often slow down in July. Many administrators plan their vacations during this time, which can result in fewer chances for teacher candidates to secure an interview. However, do not become discouraged, as interviews do still take place in July. Continue to keep an eye out for open positions as you never know what might pop up.

AUGUST AND EARLY SEPTEMBER

Hiring will pick back up in August and September as district recruiters and school administrators scramble to fill their remaining vacancies, as well as any last-minute teacher transfers or retirements. For teachers still in search of a job, anxiety and frustration builds in these months, but these feelings are normal. Use them to your advantage by doubling your efforts to find a job and looking for ways to broaden your search. Consider the following questions:

- Are you endorsed in any other areas?
- Are you willing to widen your geographical area to include other school districts?
- Are there alternative teaching positions that you could take in the interim?
- Are you willing to teach in other types of schools: alternative, charter, private, public, etc.?

As teacher candidates begin to exhaust all of their options, they often wonder, "When should I begin to worry about not having a job?" The time to worry is about one to two weeks before school starts. However, if you do find yourself in this position, do not despair, as it is imperative that you remain as positive and optimistic as you can. If all else fails, remember that it comes down to this: Schools are always in need of great teachers such as yourself, so you will eventually find the job that's right for you.

Chapter 40

Jump-Start Your Job Search

"Frustration, although quite painful at times, is a very positive and essential part of success."—Bo Bennett

As you begin your job search, it is crucial to first identify your preferences of where and what you would like to teach. Blindly entering the job market without a clear idea of what you are looking for will only prove to be a waste of time and create frustration during this already stressful endeavor. To help uncover this information, begin by asking yourself the following questions:

- What grade levels and subjects would you prefer to teach?
- What are the geographical boundaries of your job search? In other words, are far are you willing to commute each day?
- Within these geographic boundaries, to what districts and school(s) do you want to apply?

Carefully reflect on your answers to create a vision of your ideal job situation, being mindful not to narrow your focus too much. For example, when deciding what grade levels you would like to teach, list your top three choices, but also note other grade levels you would consider if certain conditions were met (i.e., closer to home, attractive benefits, higher salary, etc.). Teacher candidates are often so excited to enter the workforce that they become set on finding the perfect teaching job right out of their teacher preparation program. However, by setting this expectation, you will risk overlooking positions that may be great opportunities just because they do not fit the preferences of your ideal teaching job. Searching for the right fit is a balance; the key is to know what you are looking for and where your priorities lie while being flexible and open to different possibilities.

Armed with this new knowledge of what you want to teach, the geographic boundaries for your search, and the specific district(s) and school(s) you want to focus on, start your job search by visiting these districts' websites. Most school districts update their job openings weekly, so it is helpful to bookmark each pertinent site in your browser to save you time. Plan on visiting each site at least once a week, at a minimum, to keep up with all the current listings. Typically, school districts will keep their job listings open for only a set amount of time, which most often ranges from one week to open until filled. Therefore, if you visit the sites on an inconsistent or erratic basis, you may miss out on a myriad of job opportunities. Expand your job search even further by researching other online job posting websites, attending career fairs, and speaking to career services within your teacher preparation program or university.

Ultimately, as a first-year teacher and depending on the current job market conditions, you may have to settle on a job that is not ideal. For example, you may accept a teaching position that matches what grade level or subject area you wanted but have a longer commute than you desired. On the other hand, you find yourself in the situation of being offered a job teaching in a grade level or subject area you didn't want but in a school that is closer to home. You will have to weigh these advantages and disadvantages, but remember you do not always have to commit to the first job offer, especially if it is early in the hiring season.

Chapter 41

Attend Education Career Fairs and District Open Houses

"If you want to be seen, you have to put yourself out there—it's that simple."—Karin Fossum

Teacher career fairs and school district open houses may prove to be fertile ground for aspiring teachers seeking to improve their chances of being hired in ideal job positions. To start, these career fairs and open houses are a great way to learn more about prospective schools, school districts, and, possibly, other education-related organizations. At these events, you may glean new insights on available (or forthcoming) job openings, key initiatives centered on teaching and learning, salient community information, or other compelling insights about their organization. Keep in mind, you, as a job seeker, are interviewing employers as much as they are interviewing you. Remember that computers do not hire people; people hire people, and finding the right match matters.

Career fairs and open houses are opportune spaces to create or strengthen connections with key personnel, such as recruiters or school leaders, but remember that relationship-building takes effort. When meeting with key staff, be sure to introduce yourself, state why you are attending (e.g., "I am a teacher candidate majoring in elementary education and wondering what job opportunities are available"), and, perhaps, ask a few questions about things that matter to you. For example, you may say, "In my program, I have been learning about socio-emotional learning (SEL), and I am wondering what type of professional development your district provides for SEL." Asking questions will garner pertinent information and signal to the key personnel what type of educator you are while highlighting some of your personal passions and interests.

Another valuable benefit of attending these career fairs and district open houses is the possibility of receiving a job offer while you are there. At these events, it is not uncommon for job seekers to either be interviewed on the spot or be scheduled for a later time the same day to interview with recruiters. Then, based on a combination of factors including the applicant's qualifications, background, interview performance, etc., employers may offer letters of intent or employment contracts to interested job seekers. Be ready for this possibility by carrying plenty of résumés and a notepad for jotting down important names and thoughts. Finally, be sure to research and practice answering the common teacher interview questions (see the interviewing strategies later in this section).

Below are additional ideas to maximize your job fair experience.

- Know what you want from this experience by reflecting on what your goals are for the job fair: informational, to foster relationships, to explore alternative education careers, etc.
- Develop a plan of attack. Before attending any teacher job fair, rank the districts in attendance on desirability from least to highest. When you first arrive, start by visiting the districts/schools you have the least desire to teach in (e.g., the district is the farthest away from your home), then continue to go down your list. The value in this approach is that as you practice introducing yourself to districts that are lower stakes, you will begin to build confidence, shake off your nerves, and streamline how you present yourself to recruiters. Then, when it comes time to speak with your most desired districts, you will be less nervous and better prepared to make a good impression.
- Attend early and often. Even if you are still a year or more away from applying for a teaching position, make the effort to go and put yourself out there. By doing so, you will develop a stronger sense of what takes place at these events, initiate vital connections, and possibly find employment before you become qualified for your desired teaching job, such as a teacher candidate being offered a paraprofessional position.
- Follow up on any connections you make within twenty-four hours using LinkedIn or email. Be sure to collect business cards, or at the very least write down the names and contact information of anyone you spoke with soon after each interaction.
- Deliver on the nonverbal cues: Give a firm handshake, make eye contact, stand up straight, and smile when introducing yourself.
- Be mindful of the school or district representative's time when interacting. In other words, don't dominate their time or interrupt them if they are with another applicant.
- Dress professionally (see *Dress to Impress* later in this section).

Chapter 42

Draw from Your Network

"When shooting in the dark, it is a good idea to use a machine gun."
—Craig Bruce

Now is the time to utilize your most powerful weapon—your network. For instance, begin by reaching out to the human resource recruiters you met previously at career fairs. Remind them of who you are (and where you met them), let them know your desired teaching position, and inquire if they are aware of any positions you may qualify for. Remember to keep all communications professional, meaning that your interactions are always courteous and when reaching out via email your spelling and grammar is error-free.

Next, turn to your network of friends and colleagues. Do not shy away from sending monthly or quarterly updates on your life, and, more specifically, on the status of your job search, to your network. Ask your friends and colleagues to contact you if they hear of any teacher job openings or soon-to-be openings. A simple email here and there will suffice as friendly reminders to your network to keep an eye out for your interests.

Additionally, remember that your network serves functions beyond assisting you in finding your dream teaching job. More than likely your network includes people with whom you have authentic and meaningful relationships. Rely on those people for support and advice while nurturing those connections as well. For example, a meeting with a colleague at a local coffee shop may serve as a refreshing reminder to both of you that your job-hunting struggles are not happening in isolation. Phoning an old friend may lead to a mutually beneficial volunteer opportunity. From your professors to your cooperating teachers, it is now time to utilize your network, as you never know what doors of opportunity will open for you just by reaching out.

Chapter 43

Track Your Job Search

"Don't agonize. Organize."—Florynce Kennedy

As your job search starts to gain momentum, you may find yourself applying for numerous teaching positions, and these positions may be in a number of school districts, each with their own unique application systems and procedures. Meanwhile, you will be fully immersed in a flurry of job-related activities that include researching new job positions, submitting required application documents, and lining up your references. All of this can quickly become overwhelming and hard to manage if you are not prepared. Hence, putting into place a system to organize and track your job search activities will be a worthwhile endeavor.

A spreadsheet program such as Microsoft Excel is a simple option to organize your search. Alternatively, you can establish a free Google account that will give you access to their software called Google Sheets—a web-based spreadsheet that has the same basic functionality of Excel.

To start, format your spreadsheet to track your job search activities. Here are some sample column labels:

- Position name / Job number
- Name of school and school district
- Status / Progress (Interested, Preparing, Applied, Interview)
- List of updates with dates
- Persons you've talked with / Contact information
- To-do list

Web-based project management software and apps are another option to organize your search. Trello (https://trello.com) is an easy-to-use web-based software application that also has a useful app for your mobile device. Using Trello, you can keep on top of your search by creating lists, making cards (think to-dos), setting reminders, attaching documents, and so on.

Whatever organizational tool you choose—a spreadsheet or an app, like Trello —this tool will better help you follow up with your job search activities and reduce unnecessary and potentially harmful errors, such as forgetting to whom you spoke on the phone about an interview. Make a habit of regularly documenting all of your activities, especially after each important interaction or step you take in the application process. These simple and proactive actions will help manage all of the chaos that comes with a job search.

Chapter 44

Leverage Your Research

"The way to do research is to attack the facts at the point of greatest astonishment."—Celia Green

Before your interview, it is imperative to make a determined effort to learn all you can about your potential teaching position. School administrators are looking for job candidates who can outline specific ways they are able to contribute to the growth of their particular demographic of students. Begin by researching the local community, the school district, and the particular school to which you have applied. As a place to start, revisit the strategy *Research the Community, School, and Students* for specific research ideas and guiding questions.

As you conduct your research and glean more information, begin to identify all the ways in which you could contribute value to the school and leverage its community strengths. In other words, what kind of experience and expertise can you bring to the table? How can your specific set of skills help close certain opportunity gaps? In what ways can you fulfill specific school or student needs? Lastly, in what ways will you center the community and all that it offers in your classroom? By reflecting on and discussing these points, you will demonstrate to the interviewer the following:

- You have done your homework,
- You have analytical and problem-solving skills, and
- You are able to provide a service another job candidate may not.

Once you have gained some initial background information about the school and community, spend time getting familiar with the academic performance of your target school. This type of information can typically be found online through the state-level education government agency that oversees K–12 schools. Begin by reviewing the school's standardized test scores and analyzing the testing trends over the last few years. These scores can help you determine how well the students are doing in specific domains, and if they have shown improvement over time. Review this information with these questions in mind:

- Which subject scores (math, science, reading, writing, etc.) does the school show the most strength in compared to the district and state? Which subject scores are the weakest?
- How would you describe the overall student performance compared to the district and state?
- What data trends in the student performance strike you as interesting?
- What experiences do you have that address the school's student performance?
- What are your skills and abilities that could address some of the concerns in student performance?

Next, if you are interviewing for a secondary-level position, examine the data on how well the school prepares their students for college. Look at how many students take Advanced Placement (AP) classes and how well the students performed on the SAT and ACT tests. Further search online to identify student enrollment trends, teacher profiles, class sizes, and staffing trends in the school. Here are some guiding questions:

- What is the racial, ethnic, and socioeconomic makeup of the student population?
- What are the trends in enrollment?
- Based on the average years of teaching experience, how would you describe the staffing? Does the staff consist more heavily of novice teachers or veteran teachers?
- What percentage of the staff holds advanced degrees or National Board certification?

Another excellent source to research and from which to gain further insight is the school's website; here you can familiarize yourself with the school's mission statement and any schoolwide initiatives. While many schools do not view their mission statement as the driver of change, a few schools do take their mission statements very seriously and in an interview may ask you a question relating to this topic Now is the time to think about how you can relate the school's mission to your pedagogy. Finally, browse other information on the website for gems such as archived school newsletters that can provide valuable insight into the school's culture, strengths, and areas in need of improvement.

To help you reflect on what you gleaned from your research, draw a line down the middle of a paper. On the left-hand side, list five to ten striking findings/learnings from your research (e.g., there is an increased enrollment of English learners). On the right-hand side, jot down possible ways that you could address these learnings if they were to come up in an interview. For instance, assume you have noted the above EL student enrollment on the left-hand side of the paper. Next, on the right-hand side of your paper, write down any related experiences or professional development you have received in serving English learners. Bring these notes to your interview to remind yourself how you bring value to the students and school.

In summary, if you are in an interview and asked such questions as, "Why should I hire you?", "What makes you unique as a job candidate?", or "How will you add value to the students and school?" you will now be able to respond with focused, well-researched, and reflective responses that will be sure to impress the interviewers.

Chapter 45

Framing Your Response to Interview Questions

"In the middle of difficulty lies opportunity."—Albert Einstein

Understandably, answering interview questions can provoke anxiety and nervousness. A certain level of anxiety is expected and healthy—this unsettling feeling means you care about the position and understand the importance of your performance at the teacher interview. Too much anxiety, though, can be a self-sabotaging force. Teacher candidates may focus too much on getting the "right" or "perfect" answer, causing them to overthink while simultaneously grappling with many competing thoughts. In short, this approach is inefficient, cognitively taxing, and exhausting. Alternatively, interviewees may find themselves launching right into their response, grasping at disparate ideas and, all the while, attempting to patch these ideas together into a coherent response. Generally, they then produce an answer that lacks clarity and is often completed in less than a minute.

Applying a framework—a conceptual structure of ideas and rules—when fashioning your interview response may lower your anxiety to a healthier level and create a more coherent and compelling interview response. Let's start to unpack this framing strategy.

UNDERSTAND THE QUESTION (STEP 1)

To start, be actively listening to the question as it is being presented to you. Proceed to answer the question only if you fully understand what is being asked. If there is a part of the interview question you need clarity on, simply ask. For example, you could say, "Would you mind rephrasing the question?"

An interviewer would rather have you ask for clarification than try to improvise and give a misplaced response.

If you are confident you heard the question correctly, take a moment to think about what the question is striving to tell the interviewers about you and your pedagogy—at a higher-level. In other words, what is the essence of the question? Take as an example the following interview question: "Describe to us (the hiring committee) the first five minutes of your daily classroom routine." For this question, obviously, the interviewers are looking to hear about the specific behaviors, moves, and strategies that you will employ at the start of the school day or class period. Yet, at a higher level, this particular question is really driving at your personal approach to classroom management. The interviewers are attempting to better understand your beliefs and philosophy as it pertains to building student relationships and how you establish routines and procedures. Understanding this nuance helps you move to step 2: stating your philosophy and values.

STATE YOUR PHILOSOPHY/VALUES (STEP 2)

Your philosophy and values are reflective of your beliefs, and your values are what should guide your practice. Ultimately, teaching is really about connecting to other human beings in a meaningful and genuine way. Therefore, leaning into your values—opening up about what you stand for, what you care about, and how this motivates you—provides the interviewers a window into your authentic self. Just like teaching, you want to make a human connection during the interview process. The interviewers are not just interviewing you as a teacher but also as a future colleague.

To start your response to an interview question, make a brief statement of the philosophy and values that relate to what's being asked at the higher level. For instance, continuing with the example question above, the interviewee may respond with the following: "To start, I believe building positive student relationships and reinforcing high expectations are crucial for a high-performing classroom. This perspective will inform my first five minutes of my class." In this response, the interviewee acknowledges the essence of the question and unequivocally emphasizes the values that guide their classroom management approach.

DESCRIBE PEDAGOGICAL APPROACHES (STEP 3)

Following up on your value statement, you should then directly address the question being asked with specific approaches. Try to provide a level of specificity that creates a mental picture of your strategies/behaviors for the interviewers. And be sure to link your specific strategies/behaviors directly to the value statement. For example: "One way I will foster positive student relationships within the first five minutes is that I will greet every child with a high-five, fist-pump, or side-hug as they enter the class. Next, after the greeting, students will know they are entering into a learning community that comes with high expectations. Therefore, students will follow a routine to put away their bags, organize papers, and begin working immediately on a meaningful entry task."

EXPLAIN THE BENEFITS (STEP 4)

Next, briefly describe one or two benefits of the said strategies/behaviors. For instance, you may say, "By consistently greeting students by name, I am demonstrating to my students that I *see* them and that they are important. Also, it is a way for me to address any issues that interfere with their learning—such as if they are sad or angry—before entering the classroom."

PROVIDE A REAL-LIFE EXAMPLE (STEP 5)

Real-life examples can be drawn from a plethora of personal and professional experiences: classroom observations, work experience as a para-educator or instructional aide, volunteer work with school-age children, parenthood, and so on. This step is optional unless the interviewers directly ask you to share a real-life example. At this step, you will need to decide whether or not providing a concrete example from your experiences adds value to your response or whether it just seems like filler. Typically, I suggest providing an example when it seems as if the interviewers are seeking more information or clarity. In this case, you may want to ask, "Would you care for me to share a real-life example?" Finally, I suggest providing a real-life example when you have a compelling anecdotal story of how your described approach/strategy/behavior has positively impacted a particular student or your teaching and learnings in general.

Successfully implementation of the framework technique requires 1) knowing the framework's steps—understand the question, state values, give specific strategies, describe benefits, and, possibly, give a real-life example—and 2) practicing the application of it with various teacher interview questions. It is important to emphasize that practice is key, and the proceeding strategy *Practice Interview Questions* provides tangible ideas on how to gain more experience answering interview questions. As you practice, aim for developing an automaticity when applying the framework to respond to teacher interview questions. This method of practice and preparation will help offload a lot of the anxiety you may be feeling and, hopefully, make you more confident in responding. In short, the framework lays out a path forward to responding to teacher interview questions in a concise and thoughtful way, even when faced with the toughest questions.

Chapter 46

Practice Interview Questions

"The passion to teach is already inside your heart, but you need to secure a position you truly want and work in the district that best meets your needs. To reach that goal, you need to prepare for the interviews you will receive."—Robert W. Pollock, Ed.D.

Feeling prepared and ready for your upcoming interview is a surefire way to boost self-confidence and increase your chances of being hired for your dream teaching position. A prepared job candidate will be ready to address any question in an interview. Certainly, there will be an unexpected question or two, but the effective candidate will always be able to respond to interview questions in a thoughtful and deliberate manner. Proper preparation consists of ongoing reflection, research, and practice.

To start, reflect on your experiences and trainings that have brought you to this point. Read the reflective notes in your journal, consider the coursework and books that have inspired you, and think back on your student teaching experiences. This exercise will help you realize that you are fully prepared and worthy to start your journey as a teacher.

Next, research frequently asked questions for a teacher interview, especially for the grade level or subject area for which you are applying. A worthwhile starting point is with your career counselor and education network. Someone in your network may have knowledge of or access to the school or district interview questions. Be mindful that while some schools or districts share their interview questions, others may not. Therefore, please be ethical in your approach.

Also, you can find a comprehensive list of over one hundred interview questions in the appendix of this book. These specific interview questions were curated from dozens of educators with real-life experiences applying for teaching jobs, from all around the country. In general, most teacher interview questions typically relate to one or more of the following topics:

- Assessment
- Classroom management
- Cultural competency and diversity
- Discipline
- Family communication
- Educational technology
- Instruction
- Philosophy or your pedagogical approach
- Subject-matter or grade-level specific

    A logical next step after securing a list of sample interview questions is to practice repeatedly and often. To begin, select one to two interview questions that relate to the aforementioned topics, and jot down your how you will draft a response to these questions. Bulleting your key responses works just fine, but also consider creating flashcards with these questions and your responses to help you practice.

    Once you have created an outline of your answers for the chosen interview questions, you are now ready to start verbally practicing your responses by recording yourself. You can start by doing a simple audio recording using an audio recorder or an app (likely there is one on your smartphone or there is an audio record feature on Evernote). Record yourself reading the interview questions and reciting your responses. Feel free to reference your notes during your first few attempts, as it will help to build confidence as you practice. After each audio recording, intently listen to yourself, taking the time to analyze and reflect on the substance of your response, voice inflections, and delivery. Consider these questions:

- How satisfied are you with your response?
- Was your response succinct?
- To what degree did you show confidence and passion in your responses?
- Does your desire to teach children come through?
- Did you avoid saying "um" a lot?
- Are you speaking loudly enough for the interviewer to hear you?
- Do you convey confidence that you are the "right one" for this job?

    Continue practicing until you feel mostly satisfied and confident in your answers and are able to respond to the interview questions with a good amount of automaticity. To be clear, it may take recording yourself a dozen times or more to feel good about your response for a single interview question.

Another technique to prepare you is to videotape yourself in a mock interview. With a family member or a friend, find a quiet spot to set up a video camera to record your answers to your practice interview questions. While this may seem awkward at first, by reviewing the videotape you will see yourself from the point of view of the interviewer and catch nonverbal nuances. A further benefit to practicing with someone else is feedback. Ask your family member or friend to provide feedback on your performance. They may find something to improve on that you may have overlooked.

SUGGESTED WEBSITE

Road to Teaching: Teacher Interview Questions (https://roadtoteaching.com). This website has the largest collection of teacher interview questions.

Chapter 47

Control the Interview Process

"Those who are blessed with the most talent don't necessarily outperform everyone else. It's the people with follow-through who excel."—Mary Kay Ash

Picture this scenario. You are awaiting an interview for your dream teaching job. While nervous, you also feel self-assured in your ability to excel in this teaching position. Then the moment comes and your name is called for the interview. Immediately your heart begins pounding, your palms become clammy, and you try to hide this unpleasant reality by discreetly wiping them on your pants. You enter into the room, smile, and begin systematically shaking hands. Next, the interviewers introduce themselves, explain the interview process, and start asking questions. Eventually, the interview ends; again, you smile, shake their hands, and thank them for the wonderful opportunity. Before you know it, you are sitting in your car wondering what just happened, and questioning if it went okay. In retrospect, the whole experience seems a blur.

A few days go by after your interview, and, finally, the phone rings. The principal is calling to tell you the interview team has decided to go with someone else. The principal thanks you for your time and hangs up. You are dumbfounded. Self-doubt begins to creep in, and you ask yourself these questions:

- "Why didn't I get the job?"
- "Did I say something wrong during the interview?"
- "What could I have done differently?"
- "Am I really cut out for this?"

This scenario is problematic for a number of reasons. Namely, the interviewee left the experience in a daze because they were not in control at any point during the interview process. They simply went passively through the entire interview experience. Unfortunately, this state of wondering and self-doubt is not productive when deciding how to move forward. The key lesson in applying and interviewing for teaching positions is to understand that losing is sometimes inevitable, but the trick is not to make a habit of it. There are some simple strategies to remaining in control and wrapping up the interview in your favor.

SLOW DOWN

The first step in taking back control, and not "just passing through" the interview process, is to slow down. Pay attention to your breathing by taking deep, controlled breaths before going into the room where the interview will take place. Breathe in through your nose and out through your mouth. This technique will relax you, steady your heart rate, and put you in a better state of mind for your interview.

Another way to slow down and take control is to bring your research notes outlined with your skill sets and in what ways they match with the needs of the school. Review them just before you go into the interview as a quick reminder of some points that you should address. Taking a moment to remember all you have to offer to a potential employer can also give you a last-minute boost of confidence, which could help to further calm your nerves. When you go into the interview, and after you greet everyone, ask if you can take some notes while being interviewed. Quickly jot down the names and, if possible, the positions of the interviewers. This will be critical information for writing thank-you notes after the interview.

Throughout the interview, write down any important points made. Likewise, make a note if something you said may have caused confusion or was construed differently than your original intent. You can clarify these points later in your thank-you notes. By applying these simple acts, you become a more active and present participant in the process and less of a bystander.

PREPARE FOR PHONE INTERVIEWS

For various reasons, you may have to interview over the phone or using a video-conference service (e.g., Google Hangout, Skype, or Zoom). Here are some suggestions and hints in case you have a scheduled phone interview:

- Smile during your interview, especially in a phone interview. Smiling makes a significant difference in your tone, inflection, and speech on the phone. The interviewers will hear your smile!
- Arrange a quiet area, away from distractions, for your interview. Notify everyone not to disturb you during your phone interview and lock away any noisy pets.
- Dress professionally, especially for video-conferencing. Professional dress put you in the right frame of mind.
- Take notes during the interview—this will help you to better focus and listen.
- Have your résumé and portfolio readily available.
- Practice beforehand as if you were preparing for a face-to-face interview. Preparation is even more important if you are using an unfamiliar video-conferencing service for the first time. Try to do a trial run with a friend to acquaint yourself with the technology beforehand.

MAKE THE ASK

A relatively simple, but highly effective way to close an interview is to ask for the teaching job. In the business world, the most significant factor that contributes to substandard performance in sales is not closing the sale, or in other words, not asking for the sale. The same principle applies to interviewing. In essence, you are selling yourself: your skills and experience. Toward the end of the interview, briefly restate your desire to teach in the target school and outline the two or three reasons you are a qualified candidate. Finally, thank the interviewers for their time.

ASK A THOUGHTFUL QUESTION

Typically, at the end of an interview, you will be asked if you have any questions for the interviewers. Take advantage of this and aim to have one to two thoughtful questions ready to be asked. By asking a question or two, you can show you did research on the students, school, and community and signal that you are passionate about teaching. Consider inquiring about school or district initiatives, professional development opportunities, or beginning teacher support. Avoid asking questions that you could have easily found through some basic research.

Another question you may consider to ask is, "Do you have any concerns about my candidacy, at the moment, that I could address?" Please note that by purposely saying "candidacy" and not "me," helps make the question less personal, allowing the interviews to be more open in their responses.

This question is often unexpected and may take your interviewers by surprise. Yet, interviewers may affirmatively answer this question and, by doing so, surface concerns about your candidacy. Be ready if this happens by not becoming defensive. Instead, first, acknowledge the concern and then address the concern in a professional manner. For example, a principal may raise a concern that you live outside the district and the worry that after a year or two you will want to leave. You may acknowledge this concern by stating your long-term commitment to the school and that you are actively looking for housing in the local community. In conclusion, this question allows you to address, in the moment, any issues about candidacy versus having these concerns linger and potentially affect your candidacy.

FOLLOW UP IMMEDIATELY

Once your interview is complete, further differentiate yourself by sending out thank-you notes to all the interviewers that same day. Bring a stack of thank-you notes and several postage stamps with you to your interview. Then, immediately afterward and while the experience is still fresh in your mind, find a place where you feel comfortable to write thank-you notes, whether that place is in your car or at a nearby coffee shop. Refer back to the notes you took during the interview and make every effort to personalize each thank-you note. Mention something that will help your interviewer remember you above all the other job candidates. Here are a few suggestions:

- Address an issue that arose during your interview, especially when the topic favors your qualifications. For instance, perhaps your EL endorsement was discussed as an asset due to the rising number of EL students in the school; mention that in the note.
- Overcome objections by responding in detail to an interviewer's major concern if you were unable to address it during the interview.
- Highlight your skills or experiences that qualify you as a strong candidate and will differentiate you from other candidates.
- Finally, double-check for the correct names and spelling of the staff who interviewed you by looking up their information through the staff directories offered on the district and school websites. Next, relax; all you have to do is drop the thank-you notes in the mail and wait for the all-important phone call.

HANDLING THE PHONE CALL

The final step in the interview process is notification of whether you have received the job or if, instead, you are scheduled for a second interview. The notification usually comes in the form of a phone call, but sometimes it may be through a letter or email. Before you receive that phone call, there are steps you should take to prepare yourself.

Imagine the worst-case scenario: The principal phones you to inform you that you will not be filling the teaching position. While this is a crushing blow, take control of the conversation and learn from it. First, be extremely professional and courteous—you never know when another position may materialize at the same school. Thank the administrator for their time and ask what specifically you could improve on in the interview or on your résumé for the next time. Often the administrator will provide honest and constructive feedback. Remember to listen, and, most importantly, be receptive to what the principal is saying. It is not to your advantage to be defensive. As in the teaching process, you can take this advice, revise your approach a little, and confidently prepare for your next interview.

Now, imagine the best-case scenario: The principal phones you to offer you a position. Understand, though, often human resources cannot officially offer you the job until your reference check is complete. Therefore, it is important to have your references lined up, with primary and alternate contact numbers ready if there are any issues. Finally, thank the principal for giving you the opportunity and then, after the phone call, go celebrate—you have earned it!

Chapter 48

Go for a Trial Run

"When I have fully decided that a result is worth getting, I go ahead of it and make trial after trial until it comes."—Thomas A. Edison

Teachers prepare their students for summative assessments by using reviews, fun activities, formative assessments, and so on. Coaches condition their teams through countless drills and practices before the big game. Musicians hone their skills and technique by rehearsing their parts and adjusting after each run-through. In all aspects of life, practice builds awareness, confidence, and skills, while helping to reduce the likelihood of failure. This same principle—practice—applies to the interview process. If you tend to get anxious, sweaty, or choked up during an interview—completely natural feelings and reactions—consider going for a trial-run interview to gain insight into the interviewing process.

To effectively use this strategy, identify and apply for some open teaching positions that you would be qualified for but are not necessarily the exact jobs or in the locations you desire. By choosing less desired positions, you will take a good amount of pressure off of yourself as the stakes are lower and therefore it will be less of a big deal if you do not get offered the job. These lower stakes allow you to enter the interview more relaxed, and this may help you to focus on how to answer the questions more effectively. It will also give you the freedom to make mistakes, try out different ways of discussing your personal experiences, or test out which answers tend to make more of an impact. Plus, there is always a chance you may end up being offered the job, which you could then take into consideration and ultimately accept if it feels like the right fit for you.

As an important final note, understand that when applying this strategy, there is a professional fine line that you need to be careful not to cross. While this may just be a practice run for you, the hiring committee is really looking for someone to fill their open position. Hence, applying to positions for which you are not qualified will be unproductive for you and all parties involved. Additionally, be respectful of their hiring process by not leaving them in a lurch if they happen to offer the position to you. If you are not interested, be sure to communicate that to them as soon as possible so they can move on to the next applicant. In the end, when implemented in a professional manner, this strategy can provide you with invaluable real-life interview experience. This extra experience will hopefully help boost your confidence and better prepare you to successfully interview for the position you really desire.

Chapter 49

Dress to Impress

"Is my dress too short?"—Victoria Beckham

If you truly want the job you desire, dressing appropriately for the interview is a must. All of the hard work and hours spent creating an effective résumé and practicing interview questions will pay off only if you present yourself in a professional manner. The way you dress is not only a reflection of your professionalism, but it is also an expression of how much you care about the position you are interviewing for. Surprisingly, there have been many troubling stories of teacher candidates arriving at interviews in shorts or jeans or wearing baseball caps. Unfortunately, no matter how qualified you may be or how good you look on paper, if you are dressed unprofessionally, administrators will likely move on to the next job applicant without a second thought.

Many teacher candidates wonder just what professional interviewing attire consists of. Tables 49.1 and 49.2 have some specific guidelines to help you put together your professional interviewing outfit.

As you put your outfit together, be sure that everything coordinates. For instance, if your dress shoes are black, then wear a black belt and avoid wearing white socks with your professional attire. For women, here are some further notes on clothing that should be avoided:

- Skirts more than two inches above the knee
- Shirts showing midriffs or cleavage, or see-through clothing
- Dresses with spaghetti straps without a jacket

Table 49.1 Men's Interview Attire

Recommended Attire	Acceptable Attire
Business suit, dress shirt, tie, belt, and dress socks	Sweater, slacks, dress shirt, belt, tie, and dress socks
Sports coat, dress slacks with a dress shirt, belt, tie, and dress socks	

Table 49.2 Women's Interview Attire

Recommended Attire	Acceptable Attire
Business suit (slacks), blouse, and nylons, tights, or trouser socks	Slacks with a blouse, sweater, and nylons, tights, or trouser socks
Business suit (skirt), blouse, and nylons or tights	Slacks with a blouse, jacket, and nylons, tights, or trouser socks
Business dress with sleeves, and nylons or tights	Skirt with a blouse, sweater/jacket, and nylons or tights
Business dress with blazer, or sweater, and nylons or tights	Skirt with a blouse, jacket, and nylons or tights

ACCESSORIES, PIERCINGS, AND TATTOOS

As a final note, many teacher candidates often wonder about what is considered appropriate when it comes to accessories, piercings, and tattoos. In general, accessories such as jewelry are fine as long as they coordinate with your business outfit and are not too flashy or large. As for piercings, if it is possible, you should remove any visible body piercings other than those in your ears, which should also be limited to one or two. Lastly, if you have any visible tattoos, make an effort to cover them as much as possible up for your interview.

Chapter 50

Hit a Home Run

"Do not hire a man who does your work for money, but him who does it for love of it."—Henry David Thoreau

Hiring committees and administrators are seeking applicants who are deeply passionate about the children, community, and pedagogy. It is no secret that teaching entails work that is emotionally draining, including long hours, countless demands, and ongoing professional development all while being unfairly compensated and undervalued. Therefore, the passion and devotion you bring to the profession will be the fuel to help you overcome these challenges and push forward.

During your interview, look for any opportunities to share your why: the reasons you are seeking this position and why you are the right fit for it. In fact, you may be directly asked, "Why are you applying for this position?" but in other cases, you will have to communicate your passion by answering less-direct interview questions. Take time before going into your interview to reflect on your dedication and enthusiasm for education, especially as it relates to the students, community, and pedagogy.

One way to express your passion for teaching is by recounting a story about a particular student and their growth and describing in detail what role you played in their success. Be sure to elaborate on how these student successes motivate you to be the best teacher for your students.

Next, keep in mind the crucial role community plays in teaching and the school environment by expressing your understanding of its importance. For example, if you are from the local community, share some of your lived experiences and the reasons you want to contribute and give back to the community. If you are from outside the area you would be teaching in, share what inspires you about the community, such as the spirit of the residents, the rich diversity, or the sense of solidarity and resilience. It is also a good idea to name some specific community assets you could envision using with your students in the classroom.

Lastly, outline the reasons why you think you would be great at teaching that particular grade level or subject area by drawing on your personal experience. For example, you may be passionate about special education because a close relative has autism and you understand the importance of providing a safe and caring learning environment for exceptional children. Alternatively, perhaps you have been a math or English tutor for some years and feel a deep connection to the content and can speak to your love and enthusiasm for teaching those subjects. Wherever your passions may lie, be sure you do not leave the interview without demonstrating them in some way to the interviewers. By leaning into your commitment and enthusiasm for education, you will be able to address the interview questions with your head, heart, and soul. In the end, you only have one shot at this interview, so make it a home run!

Chapter 51

A Principal's Perspective
A Passion to Teach
Cris Welch, a Retired Elementary School Principal

You can see it in their eyes, you can hear it in their words, in their stories, and it casts an aura around them. It is one of the things I look and listen for when I interview a candidate to work with my elementary students.

In today's market, there are handfuls of excellent candidates for an elementary position. With the multitude of educational colleges that train teachers, I often wonder if they see the passion in their students. Are they able to see a fire for teaching, something that cannot be taught, but centers itself in the very core of their work? That core is passion!

We are in a time of restructuring, aligning curriculum, differentiating instruction, assessing learning, and helping young students become lifelong learners. The challenges presented daily are overwhelming, demanding, and endless. Our students come with all types of backgrounds, from the affluent to the impoverished, from single parents, divorced parents, grandparents, to not having parents. Connecting with each child and building a trusting relationship to enable the learning process is a challenge that changes with each student.

A teacher's passion supports them through these hard times. It is this inner core of strength that propels them to meet each day with purpose, belief, and dedication. It is this inner core that will help them see through the multitude of demands of accountability to what they want most for each child.

Passion is the key to resilience. Passion is the antidote for burnout, the fire that makes this job the best in the world.

Appendix
100+ General Teacher Interview Questions

ASSESSMENT QUESTIONS

- Give me an example of a performance assessment.
- Explain how you use assessments as a way to improve student learning.
- What methods have you used or would you use to assess student learning?
- What standards of measure will you use to access your students? Will you use state, national, or local standards?
- Other than tests, how do you assess student learning?

BACKGROUND QUESTIONS

- Why did you become a teacher?
- Are you a risk taker? (Give an example.)
- Are you a positive and energetic person? (Give an example to back up your answer.)
- Tell me about yourself.
- In what ways are you an empathetic person? (Give an example.)
- How can you tell that a person is a good listener?
- Are you an objective person? (Give an example.)
- What motivates you?
- What do you want to do with your life?
- What was the most frustrating thing that happened to you as a student teacher?
- What are your strengths? What are your weaknesses?
- What is the role of the principal? Does a conflict exist between your perception of a principal's role and his/her role as your evaluator?
- Describe your student teaching experience.

- During your student teaching, were you ever involved with a situation at school involving racial tension? If so, how did you handle it?
- What subjects have you taught?
- Are you patient? (Give an example.)
- Do you ever feel angry toward your students?
- What is your educational philosophy?
- If you could create the ideal school, what would it be like?
- Do you like to be challenged? (Give an example to back up your answer.)
- What do you like most/dislike most about teaching?
- How do your life experiences prepare you for teaching?
- What teams and/or clubs did you belong to as a student?
- What activities would you coach or advise as a member of this staff?
- Why did you choose to be a teacher?
- What do you like most about a teaching career?
- Describe "professionalism." What does it mean to you?
- Why should you be hired for this position?
- Tell us/me about your planning habits. If there a particular format that you use? Do you plan on a weekly basis?
- Scheduling is tricky and difficult at times. How do you approach conflicts that arise in regard to scheduling with your colleagues?
- State your educational philosophy. How do you incorporate it into your daily instruction?
- What are the three most important characteristics of an effective educator/teacher?
- Why do you feel you are qualified for the position for which you are applying?
- How would you handle difficult parents?
- What three words would your students use to describe you?
- If a student comes into school with a bruise on their face that you did not notice the day before and that student comes up to you and says, "I need to tell you something, but you have to promise not to tell anyone," what do you do?
- What does it mean to be a teacher?
- What is the ideal relationship between a teacher and student?
- What motivates you to achieve your goals to be successful?
- How would you describe yourself as a team member?
- How would others describe you as a team member?
- Why are you leaving your current position?
- Why do you want to teach in this district?
- What are some characteristics that you would find favorable when dealing with administration?
- What is a challenge that you feel you recently overcame (in your teaching career)? How did you search out resources to help you do so?

- Are there any questions you have for us
- How do you manage stress?
- Are you fluent in any language other than English?
- What else would you like to share about yourself?
- What experience have you had working with at-risk students?
- How would you deal with an uncooperative colleague?
- What would you expect your students to have gained after having you as a teacher?

CLASSROOM MANAGEMENT QUESTIONS

- If a student said she thought you were the worst teacher she ever had, what would you say?
- If a student came to you and said, "None of the other students like me," what would you tell him/her?
- How do you feel if a student does not meet a deadline?
- Do you believe you should build rapport with students? If yes, how?
- How do you feel about noise in the classroom? How do you handle noise in the classroom?
- How do you organize your classroom?
- Describe the first five minutes of your class.
- Give an example of a rule or procedure in your classroom.
- You have a child with autism in your classroom who has a hard time with transitions. How do you accommodate this child?
- Provide an example of how you handled a peer conflict.

DISCIPLINE QUESTIONS

- Some people say you should demand respect. Do you agree or disagree?
- It is the first day of class. You are writing something on the board, and a paper wad hits you in the back. What do you do? Later the same day, if all the students drop their pencils at the same time, what do you do?
- How do you handle a child who seems gifted but is a discipline problem?
- Describe your discipline plan.
- How do you curb student misbehavior?
- Describe a troubled student you have had in the past and how you helped him/her.
- How would you handle a student who constantly disrupted the learning environment?
- How would you handle a student who was cheating on a test?

PEDAGOGY QUESTIONS

- What will you do to engage parents? How will you get them actively involved in their child's education?
- How do you give your students recognition? Do you think a student can have too much recognition?
- What are various reading strategies you use?
- How would you incorporate math into your curriculum (for non-math teachers)?
- What strategies would you use to enhance students' writing skills?
- What are various vocabulary strategies you use?
- What's the difference between a good and a great teacher?
- How would you handle making a difficult phone call to a parent?
- Explain how you use differentiated instruction in the classroom.
- Describe two to three instructional tools you need in the classroom.
- What role do standards play in your classroom?
- Describe your teaching style.
- Describe your ideal lesson.
- Have you team-taught? What's your opinion on it?
- Describe a teaching strategy you used to maximize the learning potential of all students.
- How would you decide what should be taught in your classroom?
- Describe any multicultural, gender-fair classroom practices you have used in the past and the ways in which you would ensure equality among your students.
- What is your philosophy on homework?
- Describe your use of auditory, visual, and hands-on teaching techniques.
- Provide an example of a successful lesson that you created and used.
- How do you keep your students engaged 90 to 100 percent of the time?
- Describe adaptations have you used with students with special needs.
- Full inclusion is part of the educational environment. How would you meet the needs of a full-inclusion child and design a program for him or her?

PROFESSIONAL GROWTH QUESTIONS

- What are your goals for next year?
- What is the last book you read or conference you attended that benefited you professionally?
- How do you keep abreast of your field?
- What will you be doing in five years?
- What is the most significant professional development you have received?
- How do you evaluate your own teaching?

STUDENT LEARNING QUESTIONS

- How do you use technology to enhance student learning?
- How would you rank these in importance and why: planning, discipline, methods, evaluation?
- How do you encourage students to learn? Can a student be forced to learn?
- Do you make learning fun? (Give an example.)
- How do you encourage students to be active in learning?
- How do you communicate your student learning expectations?
- How do you know that your students are learning?
- How do you support 501 students' and special services students' learning?
- What is the number-one factor that contributes to student learning?

About the Contributors

Tina H. Boogren was a 2007 finalist for Colorado Teacher of the Year and received the Douglas County School District Outstanding Teacher Award eight years in a row. In addition to writing articles for the National Writing Project's *The Voice* and *The Quarterly*, she is the author of *In the First Few Years: Reflections of a Beginning Teacher*, *Supporting Beginning Teachers*, *The Beginning Teacher's Field Guide: Embarking on Your First Years*, and *Take Time for You: Self-Care Action Plans for Educators*, which was the Independent Publisher's Gold award winner in the education category. She is a co-author of *Strategies to Motivate and Inspire Students*, along with Robert Marzano, Darrell Scott, and Ming Lee Newcomb, and is a contributing author to Richard Kellough's *Middle School Teaching: A Guide to Methods and Resources* and Robert J. Marzano's *Becoming a Reflective Teacher*.

Angela Engel was the assistant director of Career Services at Central Washington University. She supported teacher candidates in preparing for the job search and connecting with recruiters from school districts in Washington State. She possesses a master of arts degree in counselor education from the University of Central Florida and is a trained facilitator in Global Career Development and the Dependable Strengths © Articulation Process. Currently, she is a career counselor in private practice in Florida. Engel serves on several local committees to support STEM/STEAM education and experiential learning in career development.

Leah Krippner, MEd, MSEd, has taught nearly three decades with the Harlem School District in northern Illinois. She currently serves as the high school media specialist and serves on the executive board of the Harlem Federation of Teachers. She frequently mentors struggling and novice educators.

Judy Longstreth earned an M.Ed from the University of Washington School of Education where she also served on the School of Education Alumni Board. For the past fifteen years, she has been a lead field supervisor for Central Washington University and has taught undergraduate courses for the elementary and highly capable learner programs. Previous to joining Central, Longstreth was a principal for eleven years in Highline School District. She has won the Washington State Christa McAuliffe Award for School Leadership.

Leann Schumacher is an elementary teacher in Issaquah, Washington. She is passionate about supporting teacher candidates on their journey from college to career and serves as a mentor for the Renton School District Teacher Academy as well as for teachers candidates. In addition, Schumacher writes for an education-based blog called "Stories From School" sponsored by the Center for Strengthening the Teacher Profession.

Cris Welch was an elementary principal for sixteen years with Spokane Public Schools in Washington State. She received her teaching and principal certificates from Gonzaga University. As an educator, she worked closely in staff development related to cooperative learning. Her passion was working to improve and support classroom instruction.

About the Author

Eric Hougan, Ph.D., was a national Board Certified teacher and mentored novice and struggling teachers. He earned a doctorate in educational leadership and policy studies from the University of Washington, Seattle. Currently, Dr. Hougan is an associate professor in the teacher preparation program at Central Washington University. As a teacher educator, Dr. Hougan is passionate to ensure that the next generation of educators reflects the communities they serve and are pedagogically strong and equity focused. Additionally, Dr. Hougan consults and serves on various education boards and work groups, locally and nationally.

www.ingramcontent.com/pod-product-compliance
Lightning Source LLC
Chambersburg PA
CBHW030140240426
43672CB00005B/209